D0342314

Dondi Scumaci's latest book, *Designed for Success,* is a must-read for every woman who desires to reach the pinnacle of her divine destiny in the workplace. Dondi presented her "Ten Commandments for Women in the Workplace" at Cornerstone Church, and the results were sensational. If you are a woman and you read one book this year, make it *Designed for Success.*

—JOHN C. HAGEE
Senior Pastor, Cornerstone Church
San Antonio, Texas

Dondi Scumaci is a breath of fresh air. Her commonsense approach to real-life challenges motivates the reader to plan purposefully, prepare prayerfully, proceed positively, and pursue persistently the destiny God has ordained for every believer. Our "King's Daughter: Becoming a Woman of God" graduates have been greatly inspired by her teachings, and so will all who pursue her insightful approach to successful Christian living in a competitive secular world.

—DIANA HAGEE
Chief of Staff, John Hagee Ministries

As a successful business owner for twenty years, I wish I had read Dondi's book when I started. Her guidance and advice are definitely necessary for success and should be appreciated by all women who read it.

—RUSTY ROBERTSON
Cofounder, RSA (Robertson Schwartz Agency)

Dondi Scumaci's book is a real "heads up" for women in leadership. Not only does she bring the value back to women in the workplace, but she also encourages and enables them to walk straight and tall in their position, plus use the abilities they've been given to meet any circumstance in their path. Leadership positions for women are tough, and they require a full-rounded person with integrity, inner strength, and compassion. Dondi presents that to women in this book.

—TERRE K. RITCHIE
Executive Director
CBH Ministries (the Children's Bible Hour)

Every young woman starting out needs to read this book. So many young women have no idea where to go when they're starting out, and this book is a valuable leg up for all women.
—JERRI TRUHILL
Member, Women of Mercury 13

I really enjoyed *Designed for Success*. I was struck by so many things—it's hard to narrow it down to just one—but Dondi really helped me identify key mistakes women make in the workforce. I now have some key skills to approach work situations positively and proactively to work toward improving them.
—SUSAN CALLAHAN
E-Commerce Catalog Manager, Nike

This is an insightful grasp of the universal dynamics of the workplace. Not only does it show you what to expect but also how to interpret what's happening when you're blazing a new trail. It's a book full of useful tools to understand the psychology of the workplace and concrete solutions to handle its constantly shifting equilibrium. *Designed for Success* will help you get to a place where you can anticipate, rather than taking a trial-and-error look back later to see what was really going on. Although geared chiefly toward the business world, those working in other venues will certainly find it helpful and, in many cases, a revelation!
—LORRAINE SENNA
Director, *The Sopranos*

This book should be mandatory reading for every woman in business. Dondi's sage advice, executive experience, and exceptional perception will speed you to the next level of success with ease and poise.
—MARSHA PETRIE SUE
Author, *Toxic People: Decontaminate Difficult People at Work Without Using Weapons or Duct Tape*

DESIGNED
FOR
SUCCESS

DONDI SCUMACI

EXcel
B O O K S
A Strang Company

Most STRANG COMMUNICATIONS/CHARISMA HOUSE/SILOAM/FRONTLINE/ EXCEL BOOKS/REALMS products are available at special quantity discounts for bulk purchase for sales promotions, premiums, fund-raising, and educational needs. For details, write Strang Communications/Charisma House/Siloam/ FrontLine/Excel Books/Realms, 600 Rinehart Road, Lake Mary, Florida 32746, or telephone (407) 333-0600.

DESIGNED FOR SUCCESS by Dondi Scumaci
Published by Excel Books
A Strang Company
600 Rinehart Road
Lake Mary, Florida 32746
www.strangdirect.com

Unless otherwise noted, all Scripture quotations are from The Message: The Bible in Contemporary English, copyright © 1993, 1994, 1995, 1996, 2000, 2001, 2002. Used by permission of NavPress Publishing Group.

Scripture quotations marked KJV are from the King James Version of the Bible.

Scripture quotations marked NIV are from the Holy Bible, New International Version, copyright © 1973, 1978, 1984, International Bible Society. Used by permission.

Scripture quotations marked NLT are from the Holy Bible, New Living Translation, copyright © 1996, 2004. Used by permission of Tyndale House Publishers, Inc., Wheaton, IL 60189. All rights reserved.

Cover Designer: Marvin Eans
Executive Design Director: Bill Johnson
Author Photograph by Samantha Foddrill, San Antonio, Texas

Library of Congress Cataloging-in-Publication Data
Scumaci, Dondi.
  Designed for success / Dondi Scumaci. -- 1st ed.
    p. cm.
  ISBN 978-1-59979-237-8
  1. Women--Vocational guidance. 2. Businesswomen. 3. Leadership in women. 4. Career development. 5. Achievement motivation. 6. Success in business. I. Title.
  HF5382.6.S38 2008
  658.4'09--dc22
                              2007038486

First Edition
08 09 10 11 12 — 987654321
Printed in the United States of America

This book is dedicated to those who have made it possible by throwing open windows of opportunity, and to those who have invested themselves in me and through me.

It is for my parents, Rick and Johnny, who are my home base, and for two special men—my husband, Scumaci, who fills my life with love and laughter, and my son, Tabor, the most precious gift God has ever given me.

Contents

Introduction

You know me inside and out, you know every bone in my body; you know exactly how I was made, bit by bit, how I was sculpted from nothing into something. Like an open book, you watched me grow from conception to birth; all the stages of my life were spread out before you, the days of my life all prepared before I'd even lived one day.

—Psalm 139:15–16

WOULDN'T IT BE wonderful if our careers came with a personal navigation system? I love the idea of a friendly voice saying, "Prepare to turn ahead." If I missed an opportunity or made a career-limiting move, the still friendly voice would say, "Recalculating route." Imagine hearing the words, "You have arrived!"

It's a nice thought, but jobs don't come equipped with a navigation package—and you probably won't find one in your employee kit. For women in the workplace, the road isn't always well marked. It's easy to miss a turn, find yourself at a dead end, lose your sense of direction, and become lost.

You may not have a navigation system, but you do have incredible potential. You were designed for success, and your work should be challenging, inspiring, and fulfilling. You have unique strengths, and your opportunities are waiting! At this point you may be thinking, "Wait a minute! My work doesn't exactly feel like that, and where are all of these amazing opportunities?"

Does this sound like you? You work hard—you are the perfect picture of reliability and responsibility. Your boss and co-workers

1

count on you. Somehow you make it all happen. Most of the time you even make it look easy.

But are you in love with your work? Are your assignments rewarding? Do you feel like you are making a real difference? Are you growing and developing new skills? Are you ready for your next opportunity? Are you recognized for your contributions in meaningful ways?

Or are you settling for less than you were designed for? How many of these workplace realities can you relate to?

- ✓ Sometimes I don't believe in myself enough—I second-guess myself and look for permission and approval.

- ✓ I don't want to let anyone down, so I keep saying yes—even when I am overwhelmed to the point of panic.

- ✓ Conflict is very uncomfortable for me, and I go out of my way to avoid it.

- ✓ Sometimes I accept what isn't acceptable. I say, "It's fine," when it really isn't.

- ✓ I have trouble asking for—or accepting—help. I think I should be able to handle things on my own, and I don't want to impose on others.

- ✓ I feel like a complete doormat sometimes, and even though I don't talk about it, I do resent it.

- ✓ There are difficult people and difficult situations eroding my confidence, effectiveness, and job satisfaction.

- ✓ I know it's important to have a professional network, but I'm not quite sure what that is and how to get one. Even if I did know, who has time for that?

- ✓ As I balance my commitments at work and at home, I put off doing the things that will help me grow and develop. After I take care of everyone else, I don't have the time or energy to take care of me.

✓ My day is a list of to dos and, quite frankly, as I look at the list, it isn't all that exciting. And, by the way, that list is growing as I read this book!

✓ I am almost positive my boss is clueless about what I actually accomplish in a day. I don't want to brag, but a little appreciation—and a raise—would be nice.

✓ I'm burned out, stressed out, and overwhelmed.

✓ I am caught up in a negative, nonproductive, and destructive situation.

✓ Sometimes I feel like I am being "set up to fail."

✓ I support the team, but I don't feel like a member of the team.

✓ Career plan? Are you kidding? Right now my plan is to get through this week.

✓ I work hard, but sometimes I feel like a hamster on a wheel. I'm running as fast as I can, but I'm not getting anywhere.

The research for this book has been such a pleasure. It has been real-time and live—more than a decade of talking to, listening to, and helping women work through the barriers. I also see myself in these pages. I can relate to the challenges and struggles on a very personal level. And it has become personal for me—this desire for women to be strong and effective and satisfied at work.

I am convinced that if you read and implement the principles set out in this book, you will experience greater success and personal satisfaction. The challenges you face in the workplace are treated here as "calls to action"—skills longing to be learned and disciplines waiting to be practiced. This book equips you to answer that call.

As you read, I hope you *feel*! I want these pages to evoke emotion. You may laugh or cry or even get angry. With that in mind, I should warn you: I am not writing to comfort you, to pat you on the head and say, "Everything will be all right, dear." It may sound more like, "Put your big-girl panties on and do something about it!"

More than anything I hope you feel understood, highly valued, and eager to begin!

As you implement what is written about in this book, you will make a tremendous difference within the organization you serve and the lives you touch. As you envision new ways of working, new approaches and possibilities will emerge, and the opportunities you have been waiting for will arrive.

This book was written for you, and I'm glad you're here. I hope you will read it, mark it up, implement the ideas, and pass it along to others.

Chapter 1

The Call to Action

Listen as Wisdom calls out! Hear as understanding raises her voice! On the hilltop along the road, she takes her stand at the crossroads.

—Proverbs 8:1–2, NLT

GOOD NEWS! YOU are not imagining it. Women do face unique, even daunting challenges at work. There really are different rules and expectations in the workplace reserved just for women. The playing field is not always even. Sometimes the rules are unspoken, and the path is not always well marked.

Some challenges are built into the workplace. These are long-standing, deeply seated attitudes, perceptions, and expectations. Other challenges are built into us—the way we are socialized, personally wired, our temperament, beliefs, skills, and abilities.

✓ *Traditionally women have been socialized differently.* While men are raised and expected to be competitive and aggressive, women are more often taught to be cooperative and passive. Many of us grow up hearing messages like, "Don't brag. Don't fight. Get along. It's important to be liked. Accessorize." Comments like these grow into beliefs and behaviors that can limit and block personal effectiveness. These messages—and the behaviors they inspire—underscore and strengthen the stereotypes already at work behind the scenes.

✓ *Women are often "hard-wired" in ways that make successful business practices less natural or automatic;* for example, many of us have inherited the caretaking gene. This may be marvelous for empathizing, connecting, and building relationships. On the other hand, the tendency to care for others can impede productivity and teach others to become overly dependent.

✓ *Women are productive and efficient. We learn to multitask and manage the to-do list. We take great satisfaction from crossing completed tasks off the list.* Here's the problem with that: In the workplace there is a higher premium on critical and strategic thinking. This creates a real deficit for women. What is valued and respected most may not be what women are most naturally inclined to.

✓ *Women tend to "accept" when they should negotiate.* Everything is negotiable. But women don't always recognize these opportunities, understand how to maximize them, or feel comfortable with the negotiation process.

✓ *Too often women underpresent their abilities and results.* We also are more likely to discuss our challenges, fears, and feelings. That means we may be more comfortable talking about our weaknesses than our strengths!

✓ *There are expectations about how women should behave in the workplace.* When we don't meet those expectations, it can create a very negative perception.

✓ *Mentoring is a critical tool for professional development, but it can be difficult for women to find female role models or mentors.* This is a frustrating cycle. There are fewer female mentors available in the workplace, and that results in fewer women being prepared for key leadership positions.

✓ *Women in the workplace are often "ladies in waiting."* We wait for others to give us power or permission. We wait for others to recognize us. While waiting patiently may be very polite, it is not a success strategy.

✓ *Women often hesitate to ask for what they need to be successful.* There are many reasons we resist asking for help. Perhaps it's difficult to articulate what we need because we haven't identified that need. Sometimes we don't ask because deep down we believe we should be able to do it without help—because asking means we haven't done our job. Finally, we don't ask for help because we don't want to impose on others.

✓ *Women become skilled at taking care of others.* We solve problems, put out fires, have all of the answers, and make it happen. Somewhere along the line we often fail to take care of ourselves with clear goals and a well-defined career plan.

Let's explore these obstacles and more—external barriers, those built into the environment, and those of our own making. Without realizing it you may be blocking, discounting, or sabotaging yourself. This sounds like bad news until you realize the barriers you are facing at work are simply skills waiting—actually begging—to be learned and exhibited.

We start by looking just below the surface. There is a definite undercurrent there. You've probably felt the pull of it. If you don't know how to swim in it, this current can drag you completely off course. Even the best swimmers are careful to understand the current. They know it can be dangerous, and they don't take it for granted.

The undercurrent is a natural part of the environment. It is workplace stereotypes.

The Care and Feeding of Stereotypes

Stop reading for a moment and list the stereotypes women face in the workplace. What do people—yes, even women—believe about and expect from women? Try to create a balanced list with both positive and negative perceptions.

On the positive side, women are thought to be better at relationships. They are called organized, efficient, hardworking, and emotionally supportive. It also is believed that women manage stress better.

You might be surprised by the data suggesting women have the natural characteristics to be very effective managers. Their warm, open communication style creates an inclusive, collaborative environment.[1] That's the good news. The bad news is these strengths can also become the seed of weakness.

Negative stereotypes characterize women as soft, passive, weak, not achievement oriented, overly emotional and sensitive, moody, needy, unavailable for relocation, indecisive, manipulative, and catty.[2] Women are classified as caretaking and nurturing, while men are more generally regarded as assertive, direct, and in control. When men are direct and straightforward at work, they are called leaders. When women are direct and straightforward at work, other words are used to describe them.

Stereotypes are exaggerations that become expectations. These notions are frustrating and confining. They become even more so when you compare them with the attributes of leadership. The chart below makes it clearer how, when you prop these preconceived notions up against what we expect from leaders, women in the workplace have a huge perception gap to fill.

POSITIVE STEREOTYPES	NEGATIVE STEREOTYPES	LEADERSHIP ATTRIBUTES
Inclusive	Caretaking	Rational
Organized	Emotional	Analytical
Efficient	Less capable	Strategic
Hardworking	Weak	Direct
Supportive	Sensitive	Visionary
Intuitive	Irrational	Competitive
Flexible	Passive	Focused
Relationship oriented	Lacking confidence	Results oriented
Collaborative	Dependent	Directive

Stereotypes may also invite a higher level of scrutiny in evaluating the performance of women in the workplace.[3] That makes perfect sense because humans are funny: they search for evidence to support what they already believe is true.

If, for example, I believe you are hypersensitive, I will be on the lookout for that. You might handle ninety-nine situations beautifully, without a flicker of sensitivity. I may not notice because that doesn't line up with my belief about you. The one time you take something personally, I will notice. That scenario becomes part of your permanent record—and we will discuss it in six months at your next performance review!

All of this means that in addition to managing relationships, tasks, skills, performance, and results, women also must manage a set of preconceived notions. It's official. Your dance card is full.

How do women typically respond to these stereotypes? One of the most common ways women try to overcome the negative perceptions is by working harder. We try to compensate for what is perceived to be lacking. Working harder may not be the best plan; in fact, that may actually reinforce the stereotypes.

The most effective response is not to *compensate* for the negatives but to *replace* them with consistent and effective disciplines. Over time we can invite others to see us differently. As you read the following examples, notice how these women—without meaning to or even realizing they are—perpetuate negative stereotypes.

Susan was recently promoted and is attending management meetings for the first time. In each meeting she furiously takes notes. She is anxious to learn from her seasoned colleagues and wants to capture every word!

After several meetings, she notices something: her male counterparts don't write much. Occasionally they lean forward, pick up a pen, make a brief note, put the pen down, and lean back. Susan, on the other hand, looks like she is the secretary taking minutes! She also sheepishly confesses that in those first management meetings, she arrived early to make coffee and stayed after to tidy up.

There is nothing wrong with making a pot of coffee, but in this situation it is not sending the right message!

Without realizing it, Susan is undermining herself. While her enthusiasm and willingness to learn is refreshing, she needs to balance her eagerness with confidence. Susan is new to the team, and she may have a lot to learn. But she is on the team for a reason—she has real value to contribute.

Jill is an outgoing, enthusiastic communicator. She is known for her energy and optimism. While she is valued within the organization, she is also limited by the perception that she does not have strong analytical skills.

Because of this generalized perception, Jill is often asked to organize employee events. She has not been asked to lead a critical project or research a serious business issue. In a way, Jill has been typecast.

When this happens to an actress, it means she has become so identified with a certain role, she is not considered for other roles. It is very career limiting!

Some women, in an attempt to break through the female stereotypes, have tried a more masculine approach. Emulating the attitudes and behaviors of men—even successful men—in the workplace does not guarantee success for a woman. In fact, this strategy can really backfire. When a woman does not act as expected, the impression is often very negative.

That explains it! When a man communicates aggressively, it is more acceptable than when a woman communicates aggressively. What a double standard! Really, it isn't that we appreciate aggressive communication from anyone. It comes down to the expectation. We accept it when we expect it.[4]

The goal is not to become less feminine or more masculine at work. It is to be mindful of the expectations, maximize your strengths, and develop leadership qualities.

> Consider Adriana. She is attractive, confident, and competitive. She has enjoyed tremendous success in what has traditionally been a male-dominated industry. I met Adriana in a crisis. She was a new manager, and her team was derailing. Productivity was down, conflict was up, and turnover was off the chart. She reached out for help to build her team and get things back on track.
>
> I realized almost immediately her staff was absolutely terrified of her!
>
> Her team described her as demanding, overpowering, and cruel. She described herself as assertive, focused, and factual. What a disconnection in perception!
>
> I asked Adriana, "What is most important to you as a leader?" Without hesitation she replied, "Respect. I want to be respected the same way as my male counterparts are respected." When I asked, "What would you say if I told you

your staff fears you?" Without batting an eye she replied, "I would say that's a very good thing."

I almost fell out of my chair. This incredibly bright woman was mistaking fear for respect! How does that happen?

Early on, Adriana decided to be a woman taken seriously in a man's business. She was determined that her success be based on results. She would not play any of the girlie games to get ahead. She adopted the aggressive communication style she saw in her male counterparts, and it backfired miserably.

A closer look at successful women in leadership positions gives us an important insight. These women have held on to their feminine qualities while developing abilities that have been more traditionally attributed to men in the workplace (i.e., confidence, assertiveness, and the ability to think strategically).[5]

While it's important to understand the stereotypes women encounter in the workplace, if we fixate on them we give our personal power away and *excuse* ourselves from success. The best plan of action is to develop a strong set of leadership competencies and deliver real value against the organization's objectives.

You aren't going to change other people or what they believe. Thank goodness that isn't in your job description. The key is to invite people to see *you* differently—and keep inviting them until they RSVP.

A stereotype runs below the surface. Look up now at what may be overhead.

Shatter the Glass Above Your Head

In the 1970s, researchers studying workplace demographics found the number of women and minorities entering the workforce was increasing. Projections were made about the workforce of the future. It was predicted this trend would continue—and they were right.

Even though women and minorities were presenting themselves

in greater numbers, the percentage in upper management and executive positions did not increase at the same rate. These groups were underrepresented in leadership positions. In 1986, this condition was given a name: the Glass Ceiling.[6]

For our purposes, let's look at how the glass ceiling impacts women specifically.

This glass ceiling is an invisible barrier that women encounter in the workplace. The ceiling allows women to climb only so far up the ladder of success within an organization. When they hit the ceiling, they can *see* further than they can actually *go*.

The glass ceiling can happen at any level of any organization, but most often you will find it in larger organizations, beginning at the management level. It is like an obstacle course or maze designed for women in the workplace.

One way the glass ceiling has worked against women is in the traditional roles they have filled at work. Women often begin their careers in staff positions. Traditionally these jobs have been relegated as female roles. They include clerical and support roles—*girl jobs*.

Men may be more likely to start in a line position. The difference between staff and line is revenue. Staff positions are nonrevenue producing, and line positions produce revenue. Typically the management career path comes up through the line. So, if a woman begins her career on the staff side, it may be harder for her to jump the track into a management position.[7]

The career path problem for women is multidimensional. On one level, women are steered toward the staff and support positions, and from there the path is not always well marked. Women may struggle to find the next step on the ladder. This is a you-can't-get-there-from-here problem. More than one woman, after presenting an impressive list of skills and experiences, has been asked, "Can you type?"

On another level, the staff positions offer less autonomy and independence. These jobs are task oriented. They invite women to be efficient, hardworking, and organized. Staff positions probably don't encourage women to develop essential leadership skills or allow women to practice skills like problem solving, decision making, and strategic thinking.

And you guessed it—the stereotypes are reinforced again!

On yet another level, it's possible for a woman to occupy the same position as a man. She can have the same title, but she would have less power and authority than her male counterparts.

Over the years, organizations have become more mindful of the glass-ceiling problem, and many of them have made great progress in honoring the diverse strengths women bring to the table. Where there is an authentic effort to break the glass, it is not a strategy to equalize the number of women in key positions—to make an appearance of valuing women. Where there is a real commitment, there also is a real strategy to create a broader and deeper pool of talent by leveraging the strengths of women in the workplace.

Organizations committed from the top to recruit, develop, and promote women clearly see the impact women can have on the business mission.

Organizational awareness and commitment will crack the glass ceiling. But the women who actually break through it are not waiting for someone to ride in on a white horse and rescue them—and they don't use the glass ceiling to explain or justify their current condition. These women know you can't wait for the organization to figure it out. You must take the initiative. And there are steps you can take right now, right where you are.

Now may be a good time to say this is not a book endorsing female activism at work! I like men. I am married to one—a really great one. My father is a wonderful man, and my son—the most precious gift God ever gave me—is a man. Some of the best leaders and mentors I've ever had were men, and I am grateful for their leadership.

The goal here is not to bash men, and these strategies are not designed to catapult you over men in the workplace. This isn't about being better than the men you work with or work for. (Men would say they have their own set of stereotypes, obstacles, and hurdles to jump, so ease up.)

This isn't even a book teaching you not to throw like a girl. Go ahead and throw like a girl. You are a girl. This is simply a book about women being better at what they do and enjoying it more.

I am hopeful that as women implement these ideas, more female mentors will emerge. In my experience they have been rare, and we need more powerful women in the workplace. We don't need to take power away from men to accomplish that. We need to create and embrace our own power.

It's encouraging to know that women can and do break through the glass ceiling. Successful strategies to accomplish that include career planning, mentoring, networking, and sponsorship. These strategies work, but here's the catch: they aren't automatic, and they probably won't walk up and tap you on the shoulder. You must seek them out and develop them for yourself.

Consider the story of Queen Esther in the Bible. This is a woman who could have reasonably excused herself from the challenge by claiming a "glass-ceiling exemption." She went from being an orphan girl to reigning as a queen! How did she break through the barriers? She lived in a time when stepping out of the traditional role could be fatal—literally!

There is much to learn from Queen Esther. When she learned of a plot to destroy the Jewish people, she was courageous and strategic. She had a sponsor, a very effective network, and a strong system of support. She prepared diligently and patiently imple-mented her plan.

Queen Esther was motivated by strong purpose, not self-promotion or self-preservation. Trace the steps of her *career* path, and you will find months of preparation, a willingness to accept guidance, and the courage to take bold action. It is also interesting to note that, in that defining moment, with everything to gain or lose, people placed complete confidence in her ability to change the course of history.

I encourage you to study the lives and work of successful women. You may find them in history or just down the hall. How did they break through? What sets them apart? What characteristics and abilities are they known for?

Make no mistake; the glass ceiling is real, and it is wrong. More often than glass ceilings, though, I discover self-erected barriers. These are the things women do—or don't do—that get in their way. It may be comforting to point to a ceiling of glass when passed by for a promotion, but that won't make you more promotable. It will make you feel like a victim, which you most certainly are not.

It is important to discover how you may be constructing virtual barriers—your own ceilings of glass. You are the only one with the power to break through these.

Take a Deep Breath, Pick Up Your Hammer, and Prepare to Shatter Some Glass

How do we create our own ceilings? We construct virtual limits when we look outside of ourselves to explain our disappointments or blame circumstances beyond our control.

Here's an example:

> Marsha works for a micromanager. The man is an absolute control freak. He questions her decisions and undermines her authority at every turn. Marsha knows if she shares her challenges or ideas with her boss, he will push her out of the driver's seat and take the wheel.
>
> She responds by going underground and withholding information.
>
> The more she withholds, the greater his need to control.
>
> The more he controls, the more her confidence is stripped away.

What makes this situation even more demoralizing is that Marsha's male counterparts are not managed this way. They enjoy a relationship with the boss marked by mutual respect. Communication between her male colleagues and the boss looks like an open, relaxed dialogue. They actually seem to like the brute.

Ultimately, Marsha receives a poor evaluation and leaves the organization. When she shares her story, she talks about her experience with the worst leader on the planet. In her version, she is the hardworking, talented employee who just couldn't take the "good-old-boys' club" anymore. She believes she was set up to fail.

Marsha's example is common. She is looking outside of herself to explain a painful and disappointing outcome. What would have changed if she had asked these questions instead?

- ✓ How can I invite my boss to trust me more?

- ✓ What am I doing or not doing that might trigger the need to overcontrol?

- ✓ What can I do to make micromanagement unnecessary?

- ✓ How can I improve communication with my boss?

- ✓ How am I contributing to this destructive cycle?

The answers may have been:

- ✓ Communicate more!

- ✓ Build trust!

- ✓ Ask for feedback and give feedback.

- ✓ Consult a mentor—someone who is not knee-deep in this swamp.

✓ Put down your weapons and partner with your boss instead of competing with him.

Looking back on this experience, Marsha now realizes she became so focused on the ineffective behaviors of her boss that she lost sight of the real business objectives. Her goal became to "beat" her boss at some dysfunctional game of control. (Incidentally, dysfunction always invites dysfunction. You do not have to RSVP.)

Please don't misunderstand. I am not blaming Marsha for her boss's poor leadership. I applaud her willingness to accept personal responsibility for her reactions and responses. She now realizes how she contributed to the problem. That kind of personal reflection takes courage and maturity. It also pays huge dividends. What was the most painful and disappointing experience of her professional life has become one of the most valuable lessons. When she allowed it to, it made her better.

Are you facing a situation at work that leaves you feeling power-less, frustrated, or resentful? I encourage you to begin taking back your power by focusing your energy on the goals of the business and what you can do to positively impact them. In the chapters to come, you will also learn how to confront ineffective behaviors in others and how to ask for what you need to be successful.

By the way, if you see yourself in Marsha's boss, please understand your need to control is absolutely devastating to your employees! It erodes trust, undermines confidence, and destroys morale. The need to control is fear based, and your sense of control is an absolute illusion! The more you attempt to control others, the more creative they will become at going under, over, and around you. I urge you to replace your need to control with leadership.

Beware of Overused Skills

It is quite possible—even likely—you have an overused skill. Most of us do. These are skills we are particularly fond of because they have been a source of identity, recognition, and promotion.[8] At one point in your career, these skills may have been the key to your success. Proceed with caution!

Overused skills become liabilities. What a paradox! What was once a key unlocking doors of success can, without warning, become a barrier—slamming and barring those doors.

Detail orientation is a strength until it becomes overdone. Then it is called perfectionism, nit-picking, a waste of time, and *downright annoying.* Being open to the ideas of others is marvelous, but when overused, it looks like you are approval seeking with the inability to take a real stand.

> Sharon is a supervisor who cares a great deal about her co-workers and direct reports. She is sincerely interested in their work and their lives. Sharon encourages people to share their ideas, concerns, and problems with her. She listens attentively and acknowledges what is important to them. Sharon's door is always open, and her employees describe her as approachable and kind. As positive and nurturing as all of this may seem, Sharon's concern for people has become a liability.
>
> She has difficulty being firm when she needs to be, and people regularly take advantage of that. Instead of getting results, Sharon gets excuses. She is too deeply involved in the personal lives of the people she works with, and this prevents her from confronting performance issues. Sharon finds herself protecting her people instead of managing them. Her results reflect this, and she is losing credibility with her boss.
>
> Sharon's concern for people became overdone. It is now her Achilles' heel. Her strength became her seed of weakness.

We also overuse skills when our role changes and we continue to rely on an old set of skills. The skills that bring you to a new position will not make you successful in it. Perhaps at one point in your career the ability to organize and prioritize was absolutely essential. Then you were promoted.

In this new place and space perhaps it will be more important to delegate. That doesn't mean organizing and prioritizing are irrelevant or unimportant, but those skills won't be the key to success in your new role.

In the book *The Leadership Pipeline: How to Build the Leadership-Powered Company,* authors Ram Charan, Stephen Drotter, and James Noel teach us that each time we make a career transition, three things must change:

1. How we use our time

2. What we believe is important and focus on

3. The skills we need to be successful

Here the career path is not imagined as a wide, sweeping road to the top; it looks more like hard right and left turns—switchbacks on a narrow highway. If we don't shift, we may have a new job title, but we don't really make the turn.[9]

What is your favorite key? Are you using it too much? Has your role changed, and are you still relying on an old set of skills?

Perhaps you are feeling typecast. You are ready to take on more challenging and exciting assignments, but you aren't even being considered for them.

This is your turning place. Here awareness meets ability, and you will have the opportunity to make positive changes in your course.

We've laid the foundation with some of the common issues women face at work. We've looked behind the scenes and below the surface to understand these challenges more.

In the chapters to follow, you will learn how to confidently navigate your workplace challenges and how to maximize your opportunities.

You will be introduced to what I call the Ten Commandments for Women in the Workplace. These commandments offer insights, skills, disciplines, and best business practices. As you study the commandments, you will see problems that are unique to women in the workplace. You will be able to trace the symptoms, understand the causes, and see the impact these problems have on women. At the end of each chapter you will find high-impact ideas, questions for personal reflection, and recommended action items. You will be able to:

✓ *Use the high-impact ideas to build momentum and get traction.* These ideas summarize and reinforce the concepts you just learned.

✓ *Consider the reflective questions as truth-telling opportunities.* Use these opportunities to gently—or not so gently—tell yourself the truth about where you are in your career and what needs to change.

✓ *Use the action items as ways to personally apply what you've learned.* Then implement the items relevant to your situation. These actions are an opportunity to practice—to stretch. As with any stretching exercise, you may feel some discomfort. Remember, comfort is not the goal!

As you make your way through these pages, I encourage you to treat it as a journey. Enjoy the process! Journal your progress as you go—create milestones and monuments that mark your progress to remind you how far you've come.

High-Impact Ideas

✓ Some of the challenges women encounter at work are built into the environment. Others are built into us. Being aware of environmental barriers is helpful, but fixating on them isn't. Focus on the things you can change—you and how you respond to the barriers in your path.

✓ There is a significant gap between female stereotypes and the attributes of leadership. Build leadership qualities, and let the stereotypes take care of themselves.

✓ The goal for women at work is not to compensate for negative stereotypes by simply working harder or becoming more masculine in their approach. Be mindful of the perceptions and expectations, and manage your responses.

✓ Study the lives of successful women. You will find that they held on to their feminine qualities while developing abilities that have been more traditionally attributed to men in the workplace.

✓ The glass ceiling is real. But the virtual barriers we construct are probably more common. And we have greater control over them.

✓ We must take responsibility for our own development. While many organizations are committed to breaking the glass ceiling by recruiting, developing, and promoting women, we cannot rely on that.

✓ Prepare yourself for key leadership positions. Mentors, sponsors, and a strong network are key strategies for women in the workplace.

✓ Take responsibility for your own actions. We give our power away and construct virtual limits when we look outside of ourselves to explain our disappointments or blame circumstances beyond our control.

✓ It is quite possible, likely even, that you are overusing a skill. What was once a key to your success can—without warning—become your Achilles' heel.

✓ The skills that bring you to a new position will not make you successful in it. When your role changes, the skills you need to succeed must also change.

Questions for Reflection

What barriers or challenges are you facing at work?

_____

_____

_____

How are you responding to these obstacles now?

_____

_____

_____

What needs to change?

_____

_____

_____

Action Items

Review the list of typical stereotypes and evaluate yourself. Are there ways you are unintentionally reinforcing those negative perceptions? What are those ways?

When you encounter a barrier or an obstacle, resist the temptation to look outside of yourself to rationalize or explain it. Focus instead on your own responses and your objectives.

Take a personal skills inventory. What are your greatest strengths? What skills do you need to focus on? Which skills may be overused?

Chapter 2

COMMANDMENT 1:
Manage Your Message From the Inside Out

IMAGINE THAT WHEN you were born, you were given a box. The box is empty to begin with, but almost immediately people begin to put messages into it. Some of the messages make you feel strong and safe and powerful; others teach you to doubt yourself and your abilities.

Over time the box is filled with messages. Some are duplicates. You've received them more than once and from more than one person. One message tells you it's important to be popular, one reminds you to always be very polite, while another tells you to wait to be recognized—because bragging is very bad. Your messages warn you against making mistakes, rocking the boat, or being *pushy*—because nobody likes a bossy girl.

Now imagine shaking the box! The messages get all mixed up. That makes it hard to separate the encouraging, empowering messages from the negative, limiting ones.

You grow up and carry your box of messages to work. As you begin to use them, you discover that, for much of your life, the messages have been managing you. Now you must learn to manage them.

25

Communicating powerfully can be a real struggle for women. We are socialized to develop less confidence, to be less independent, and to undervalue our capabilities and intelligence.[1] Even so, women can be dynamic communicators. You can be a dynamic communicator! This is exciting, because everything you do to improve your ability to communicate impacts your relationships and your results.

Communication is the cornerstone of personal effectiveness, and it's an inside-out job. What begins as an internal dialogue—what we believe about ourselves, say to ourselves, and expect for ourselves—becomes how we present ourselves to others. This presentation is both spoken and unspoken. We are always communicating—with or without words.

How we present ourselves becomes what others believe about us. And what others believe about us and our abilities shapes their responses to us. Finally, the responses we receive from others come back around to reinforce the original belief.

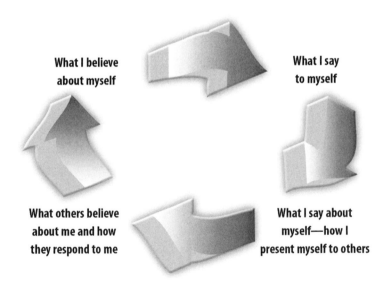

As you can see, the cycle begins with what you believe about yourself and becomes what others believe about you and how they respond to you.

By way of example, let's say I believe I cannot speak in front of a group. What I say to myself is: "You will look ridiculous. Your brain will fall right out of your head in front of everyone. You'll probably trip and fall." As I torture myself with thoughts like that, I step to the front of the room. I don't feel confident, and I don't look confident. With a trembling voice, I apologize to the group with an opening statement like, "Please bear with me. I am very nervous."

I fail to engage others with my presentation. If anything, they are embarrassed for me—this pitiful creature fumbling around with her notes and looking as if she might run from the room at any moment.

After the presentation—as I am remembering everything I should have said—I continue to torture myself, thinking: "What a disaster. They hated it. I cannot speak in front of a group."

The belief that limited me now has a stronger hold on me. And I've invited others to believe it, too.

Release Your Internal Brake

We all have them—beliefs, even unconscious ones, that hold us back. This is a little like driving down the freeway, seventy miles an hour, with the emergency brake fully engaged. You may be getting somewhere, but you are most certainly tearing up the car. The instructions in the owner's manual should read: "Locate the beliefs that limit you to release your inner brake."

When I began speaking professionally, I learned the hard way how beliefs impact performance. One of my self-limiting beliefs was: "It's very important for people to like you—to approve of you." With practice, I could take this belief to a whole new level: "It's the most terrible thing in the whole wide world if people don't absolutely love you, and they might not."

This belief drove my performance. Above anything else I desperately needed *everyone* in *every* audience to like me. I could receive thundering applause and wonderful feedback, but if I had one mediocre evaluation or if I didn't "feel the love," I would instantly turn that into a weapon and torture myself all the way home.

This is ridiculous behavior—really ridiculous and really painful behavior.

The obsessive need to be liked became the primary focus of my performance. It was like a drug. I was an approval addict, and my performance suffered.

I continued to struggle with this behavior until I identified the belief driving it. Then I understood: "It's not about people liking you. In fact, it's not about you at all! This is about them. It is about making a real difference."

With an audible sigh of relief, I mentally crossed out the rule "It's important to be liked" and replaced it with "It's important to make a lasting difference." I was free then to focus on the audience and on making a positive impact. I enjoyed my work more and my performance improved.

How do you locate your self-limiting beliefs?

Begin with what you believe about your accomplishments, strengths, and abilities. What are you really good at? What achievements are you most proud of? What skills have you mastered?

Start with what you believe about yourself, and then listen to what you say to yourself.

The Critic Living in Your Head

Do you talk to yourself? Of course you do. We all do. Have you listened to that conversation lately? I dare you to keep a log of your self-talk for one week. You may be shocked at how mean you are to you!

The first step in managing your self-talk is to become more aware of it. This conversation has been going on for so long in your head, it's like background noise—elevator music! You don't even notice it anymore. Turn up the reception and really listen to what you are saying. What do you say to yourself when:

✓   You make a mistake?

✓   You look in the mirror—naked?

✓   You forget something important?

✓   You say the wrong thing?

Once you have isolated the negative messages, replace them with positive, empowering ones. Imagine for a moment that your self-talk is like programming a computer. You are either programming yourself for success or failure, and your thoughts are like commands. Software designers know that a bad command in the program cannot be ignored. Until a bad command is replaced, it wreaks havoc in the program.

Our words have such power—more than we may ever realize. It is true, "Death and life are in the power of the tongue" (Proverbs 18:21, KJV).

Never say anything to yourself or to anyone else that you do not sincerely wish to be true.

When you catch yourself saying, "I am so stupid," stop! Delete that message and replace it immediately. Tell yourself instead, "I am bright and intelligent and a fast learner."

Managing your internal dialogue is so important because you cannot be a dynamic, confident communicator when you are tearing yourself apart from the inside out. It is also important because that isn't just a critic living inside you—it's a prophet. As Stephen Covey teaches in *The Seven Habits of Highly Effective People*, all things are created twice. We create them first mentally, then physically.[2]

There Is a Prophet Inside of You Predicting the Future

You will also find self-limiting beliefs by taking an inventory of your expectations. When you try something new, do you expect to succeed? When obstacles block your path, do you expect to prevail? When something wonderful happens, do you expect it to last?

29

Have you ever said, "This is too good to be true," or "This won't last"? What you are really saying is, "I can't believe this is happening for me because I really don't believe I deserve it. I am not worthy of this good thing."[3]

> Several years ago at a conference on the West Coast, I noticed a group of women sitting in the middle of a large audience. They were from two local hospitals. I learned the hospitals were merging—all of these women were in a very vulnerable place. Some of them would not have jobs when the two organizations folded together.
>
> One woman in particular caught my eye. She was so engaged—so full of energy. On a break she introduced herself and a colleague. She was almost breathless when she said, "I am excited and terrified! My job at the hospital may be eliminated. This situation is pushing me way out of my comfort zone. For the first time in years I am thinking about what I would love to do."
>
> Her optimism was compelling and contagious. Then her associate spoke: "Yeah, you work for a company for twenty-five years, and they kick you to the curb six months before you retire." You could almost hear the vacuum as the oxygen was sucked from the room.
>
> About five months later I received an e-mail from the first woman. She was writing to tell me exciting news. She had received a significant promotion with the merged organization. She was absolutely thrilled with her new job. I was not surprised.
>
> When I wrote to congratulate her, I couldn't resist asking about her colleague. She replied, "Oh. Unfortunately she was in the first round of layoffs." Again, I was not surprised.

What is more tragic than this woman losing her job was that she left the organization believing that something had been done to her.

Here you have two women in the same situation experiencing very different outcomes. What accounts for the difference?

One of them made empowered, accountable choices. One of them behaved like a victim. Both of them had a prophet inside predicting the future. Both of the prophecies came true.

You will find the beliefs that are limiting you by noticing what you believe about yourself, what you say to yourself, and what you expect for yourself. You release the internal brake by reflecting on your abilities, firing the critic, and managing the prophet.

This is where your communication turns from inside out. Next we will look at what you say about yourself—how you present yourself to others.

Marketing vs. Modesty

Early in my career I received this advice: make your progress visible and your results obvious. I would add something to that now: make your progress visible, your results obvious, and your story compelling.

This is a marketing message, and for many women it feels awkward and uncomfortable to talk about their achievements. We are taught not to brag, and this definitely feels like bragging!

You probably won't be surprised to learn that women tend to underestimate and underpresent their results.[4] In fact, women even tend to explain achievement differently. When women succeed, we often attribute it to luck. When men succeed, skill is to blame!

> Margaret just spent her entire weekend working on an important presentation. After the meeting, her boss congratulated her on an outstanding performance. Margaret throws the positive feedback to the wind by highlighting a weakness in the presentation: "Oh! Do you really think it was all right? I was so upset with the typo on page three, but nobody seemed to notice. Whew!" The underlying message is: "I'm not that good. I'm just really lucky."

Margaret missed an opportunity to gracefully market herself. She might have said, "I worked very hard on this presentation. Thank you for noticing."

Psychologists once believed women present themselves modestly because of low self-esteem and a lack of confidence. That is certainly a factor, but research also gives us an alternative explanation.

Women want to be liked. To that end we may use modesty and self-depreciation as a communication bridge—a connection. Women also tend to overestimate the credentials and experience of others while discounting their own.

> I watched this scenario play out with one of my dearest friends. She is dynamic and beautiful, hardworking and extremely talented. For more than twenty years she has been a successful businesswoman in the Pacific Northwest. Recently an opportunity was presented to her. Her response is a prime example of how women underestimate themselves and overestimate others.
>
> My friend was asked to consider joining a large organization because of the creative, intuitive way she works with her clients. While she does not have a formal degree in this field, she has an amazing God-born talent and decades of successful experience. As she investigated the opportunity, she began to question her qualifications. "I don't have the formal training for this. The people in this company have incredible résumés." I gently—OK, maybe not so gently—reminded her that her own résumé was nothing short of incredible.

My dear friend did what many of us do. We supersize the value of others, but when it comes to our own value we think in terms of the kid's meal!

We have all been turned off by people who are walking, talking, look-at-me billboards. This is not marketing. It is ill-timed, attention-getting, out-of-context trumpeting. The noise of it does not compel—it repels.

At the opposite end of the spectrum is complete obscurity—a lack of clarity, distinctness, and definition. Perhaps the answer is found somewhere in the middle—a gentle balance of humility and confidence, understanding when and how to communicate a sincere, authentic message that sells.

I love this quote from Peggy Klaus in her book *Brag! The Art of Tooting Your Own Horn Without Blowing It:* "Learning to brag is not about becoming something you aren't or trying to put something over on someone. In fact, bragging as an art is just the opposite. It's about becoming more of who you are and bringing forward your best parts with authenticity, pride, and enthusiasm. It's about telling your story in a way that showcases your strengths. It's a way of building a bridge to others and to better opportunities."[5]

Instead of marketing themselves, many women wait for the recognition to come. They mistakenly believe that if they just work hard enough, someone will notice. And *someone* might. But it might not be the *right* someone.

Working hard and doing exceptional work won't be enough. You must make your efforts and results visible. You must learn to think like a marketer and sell your story. Here are eight tips for marketing yourself graciously:

1. Instead of talking about what you did, talk about the difference it made.

2. Instead of talking about what you can't do, talk about what you can do and what you are learning to do.

3. Talk about your goals and how you will measure your success.

4. Debrief results with your boss candidly and without apology. Listen to the difference between these two approaches: "I think the project went all right. There were some rough spots, but we made it through." Compare

that report with this one: "We met our objectives, and we learned a great deal. I am most proud of the way we…"

5. Quantify your results whenever you can. Instead of saying, "I think we will save a lot of money," say, "I estimate a savings of more than $10,000."

6. When you fall short of your goals, ask for feedback, and talk about what you have learned from the experience and how you will apply those insights in the future.

7. Talk about your weaknesses differently. Instead of saying, "I need to be more analytical," say, "I want to strengthen my analytical skills. What projects or assignments would help me do that?"

8. Even your challenges are opportunities to demonstrate creativity and problem-solving skills. When you aren't getting the results you need, present the issues along with your recommendations and solutions.

Prepare for Your Openings

Opening night on Broadway happens after weeks of exhaustive practice and rehearsal, making even the most difficult performance look effortless and completely natural. You have openings, too. They may happen at any time. Prepare for them with marketing messages.

The most effective marketing messages are carefully constructed and rehearsed. They are not off-the-cuff, fly-by-the-seat-of-your-pants speeches breathlessly delivered in the elevator. These are thoughtful messages highlighting your accomplishments, results, experiences, and contributions. These messages are chapters in a larger story—the story of who you are, what you have learned, what you do well, and what you value.

To build your messages, write down your:

1. Ten most significant accomplishments and achievements—yes, you do have ten!

2. Strengths and abilities—what you do well

3. Experiences and, more importantly, what you learned from them

4. Goals and aspirations

5. Projects you are working on now and the difference they will make for the organization—how they will directly impact the mission, vision, and bottom line

6. Interests and hobbies

7. Commitments to social or community initiatives and why you chose to support these causes

When you polish and put these messages together, you will have a story that reflects the best of you and expresses your passion. When people ask what you do for a living, what you are working on now, or why you chose this job, this story replaces what you've been saying—which, if you will admit it, has typically been your title, a department, or the organization you work for. This is not what you do or who you are!

You may be surprised how difficult this task is, and that reinforces the importance of working through it. If it's hard to think of these pieces, you most certainly aren't talking about them, and that means you are missing opportunities to market yourself. Begin preparing your marketing messages by developing five important stories:

1. What do you do?

2. What are you working on now?

3. What accomplishments are you most proud of?

4. What are you learning?

5. Where do you see yourself in the future?

Your story is a part of communication you can plan for—a piece you can maximize and manage. These are the answers that can, and should, be on the tip of your tongue. Take advantage of that, because some answers won't be.

Relax! You Don't Have to Have Every Answer on the Tip of Your Tongue

A young woman—an industrial engineer, no less—in one of my seminars recently admitted she is terrified of public speaking. I asked her why this was so troublesome for her. She said, "I am so afraid someone will ask a question about my area of expertise and I won't have the answer."

Is that really so terrible?

But for women in the workplace it can feel pretty terrible. Women believe they have to work harder to get ahead and stay there. They also believe they have to have the answer or they lose ground.

Good news: it is perfectly OK to say, "I'd like to give this more thought. I'll get back to you." It can also be so refreshing when people say, "What a great question. I'm not sure, but I can certainly find out."

When you think about it, do you really expect others to have every answer, every time? I'm betting you don't. And I encourage you to give yourself the same consideration.

Self-Disclosure or Self-Sabotage?

We know that women communicate to connect—to create understanding and build relationships. To that end, we may be more willing to talk about our fears, feelings, and challenges. We use self-disclosure to make our connections more meaningful. We pull off our "masks" and make ourselves vulnerable to others. This makes us authentic and real. Our self-disclosure invites others to pull off their masks and be authentic and real with us.

In the right moment, self-disclosure can be a powerful communication tool. In the wrong setting, it is self-sabotage! In some situations, the willingness to throw up your hands, ask the question, and admit, "I don't get it," is like a breath of fresh air. In the wrong situation, it may create a perception of weakness or a lack of awareness.

Women are socialized to be more comfortable showing emotions, while men are taught to control emotions.[6] Studies have even shown that women are more comfortable asking questions in front of a group, while men are more likely to search for the answer privately.

Use self-disclosure wisely and purposefully. Consciously choose when and with whom you will make yourself vulnerable. Use questions strategically as well. Before asking a question in front of the group, there are some things you may want to consider.

✓ Is this question timely and relevant?

✓ Am I asking this question because I really need to know or because I really need to connect?

✓ Is this a question or self-presentation?

✓ Does this question move the conversation forward or take the group off task?

✓ Do I need the answer right now, or can I make a note of it?

✓ Does my question reflect a desire to understand or a lack of preparation or awareness?

When it comes to self-disclosure, you'll want to carefully consider how much personal information to share in professional settings. Remember, the stereotypes have been working at your organization a whole lot longer than you.

Melanie, a dynamic young professional and one of the best mothers on the planet, offers this advice: "If you bring your personal *stuff* to work and have a constant stream of issues and family problems, you'll create the perception that your plate is too full. You'll be seen as someone who is not focused at work, and you won't be considered for more challenging responsibilities."

The Struggle Between Two Poles

Because women are naturally socialized to be passive, assertive behaviors can be very uncomfortable—even excruciating. It's common too for women to bounce between two ineffective poles—passive and aggressive.

Passive communicators are indirect. They tiptoe around the message until there isn't one. Passive communication looks like low self-esteem or, even worse, apathy. That doesn't mean you don't care. It means you look like you don't care, which isn't much better. It sounds like silence, agreement, or being overly apologetic.

Passive people avoid conflict, keep the peace, and meet the needs of others, but they often fail to get their own needs met.

Do you recognize this scenario? You say yes when you should say no, "It's OK" when it really isn't, and "I'm fine" when you aren't. These passive responses allow you to keep the peace and avoid a conflict, but there is a cost.

When we are passive, we aren't honest about our needs, and we teach people to take advantage of us. Each time we are passive, we leave a little piece of ourselves behind. Eventually we will resent that—and we will punish you.

Passive behavior builds until we might just snap someone's head right off! We go from passive to aggressive like a very fast car. (You have to admit this is pretty crazy behavior.) Or maybe we don't ever become aggressive. Maybe we become a martyr instead. Then we tell ourselves, "I won't say a word. I'll just suffer in silence. In fact, I may never speak to you again."

Aggressive behavior is just the opposite. It is overly direct, loud, intimidating, emotional, and demanding. Aggressive communication sounds like blame, and it looks angry. Aggressive people get their needs met at the expense of others.

Abraham Maslow said, "If the only tool in your toolbox is a hammer, you will tend to treat every problem as if it were a nail." Aggressive communication is like that—hammers and nails.

Sometimes women tell me they are passive at work and aggressive at home. Here's what I think that means. If I am passive at work, I give my power away. I am aggressive at home to take my power back. The problem is, I am taking my power from the wrong people!

Bouncing between these two poles is exhausting, and it damages your relationships and your credibility.

Perhaps you are situationally passive. In certain situations or with specific people you feel less confident, and that comes through as passive communication. I absolutely guarantee you will not build confidence or credibility by becoming passive in those moments!

Another problem for women in the workplace is when an attempt to become more assertive actually looks like aggression. This is difficult because of the stereotypes we discussed in the first chapter. Women are expected to be passive. And when they aren't passive, it can create a very negative impression.

The most effective communicators are assertive. This is a firm, factual, problem-solving communication choice. Assertive communicators fix problems. They don't place blame. They respect others, and they respect themselves. They are honest about what they need, they are concerned about the needs of others, and they use facts—not emotions—to make their point.

I encourage you to practice assertive communication, even if it feels uncomfortable at first. Read on to find dozens of ways to become more assertive and more effective with your communication.

Put a Positive Frame Around Every Message

Making your message positive is not a call for a Pollyanna, everything-is-so-wonderful approach. That is unrealistic, inauthentic, and just plain annoying. Sometimes things aren't wonderful. Sometimes things are absolutely awful. Even then you can frame your messages positively by talking about:

✓ What you want instead of what you *don't* want

✓ What you can do rather than what you *can't* do

✓ What you are as opposed what you *aren't*

Listen closely, and you will notice how often we talk about what we don't want! We do this to children when we say, "Don't get dirty." "Don't be late." "Don't get wet." Instead, why don't we say, "Stay clean." "Be on time." "Stay dry."

Pay attention to how often people talk about what they can't do. You will hear things like, "That's against the policy." "We can't do that." "That's not possible." How much more compelling to say, "Our practice *is* . . ." "Here's what I *can* do. . . ." "Here's how I *can* help. . . ." There may be one hundred fifty things you can't do in a given situation. Talk about the one thing you can do!

Finally, talk about what you *are*. I am stunned at how often people put a negative spin on a positive message. When someone asks you how you are, do you say, "I can't complain"? Or do you say, "I feel great!" When a colleague thanks you, is your reply, "No problem"? Or do you say, "My pleasure"?

> I met Kim in a crisis. I had shipped materials ahead for a conference on the East Coast. When I arrived, the materials had not. (To my knowledge they still haven't, so if you happen to see that box, please send it my way.)
>
> In walked Kim. She absolutely oozed insecurity and self-depreciation. She looked as if she were folding in on

herself—making herself smaller so as not to take up important space.

I asked Kim for help. I needed hundreds of copies in a very short time. She not only made it happen, but she also made it look easy.

When I thanked her for saving the day, she literally said, "It's no big deal." I grabbed her face in my hands—yes, I did!—and looked her squarely in the eye and said, "Kim, it is a big deal. It's a really big deal to me and to every person who will arrive shortly expecting to learn something. It is important, and you made it happen, and I thank you."

I hope all the Kims who read this will begin to understand and accept your real value.

I've become a collector of signs and phrases. I am always looking for good examples of positive and negative communication frames. I'll pack them and take them with me if they will fit in my carry-on!

The one that delights me the most is often found in hotels. Have you seen this sign? "All of the items in your room have been carefully inventoried. Any missing items will be added to your bill."

That makes me want to take a towel.

Listen to the difference when you put the message in a positive frame. This sign was found in the pocket of a hotel bathrobe: "This bathrobe has been provided for your comfort and convenience during your stay. If you love it and would like to take it with you, please let us know. We will be happy to wrap it and include it on your final statement."

Isn't the difference amazing? One message dares you to steal; one invites you to buy. One makes you an enemy; the other makes you a customer.

I found another great example on the inside of a very dirty window in Manhattan. This was a dry cleaner, and the hand-scrawled sign said, "We close at 9:00 p.m." I wanted to quietly replace the sign with one that said, "We are *open* until 9:00 p.m." Unfortunately I could not. It was 9:05 p.m.

Think of it this way: the words you choose are like a compass. Send people in the direction you want them to go.

It Is Absolutely Not OK to Cry

Regardless of what your mother told you, it is not OK to cry at work. That's what the ladies' room is for. So if you must, go in there, bar the door, and have yourself a really good sob. Don't get me wrong. *Crying* isn't a mistake. Crying *at work* is.

> Sandy has been with her organization for almost twenty years. She is dedicated and very capable. Sandy has weathered leadership changes, budget constraints, and a challenging workload. She is an absolute rock—until today when she fell apart in her performance review and burst into tears.
>
> Her boss pushed a box of tissues toward her and silently checked the "emotional woman" box in his head. Another stereotype conveniently confirmed.
>
> Sandy's situation is not unique. She has a boss with a very different working style than she is accustomed to. From the beginning, there has been an unspoken tension between them. Sandy has been on an emotional roller coaster for nine months, dreading the day of her performance review. She knows her boss is not satisfied with her work—she can sense it. She hasn't slept since the appointment was set for her evaluation, and her worst fears were realized. She received a very poor performance rating.

I've met many women in Sandy's scenario, and as I speak with them, they describe an almost surreal feeling. They can't believe they are in this position! Most of them have an employee file filled with excellent performance reviews—a career full of recognition and accomplishment. All of them have something else in common—

they failed to manage their feedback, they avoided conflict, and they mentally rehearsed failure.

What could Sandy have done to change the course and alter this outcome? Is it too late for her to recover?

Sandy could have managed her feedback more proactively and confronted the tension between her and her boss more productively. She wasn't comfortable initiating these conversations, and now her ability to recover depends on her willingness to step out of her comfort zone. In chapter 4 you will learn how to go get your feedback.

When You Avoid Conflict, You Incubate It

Conflict can be so uncomfortable, and we may be so tempted to push it under the rug. The problem with that plan is, eventually you will be tripping over all the bumpy rugs. It's a paradox—when you avoid conflict you actually incubate it. It grows. Even if conflict is excruciating for you, there are ways to manage it more effectively.

In Sandy's case the conflict is unspoken—a silent, paralyzing tension building between her and her boss. When faced with conflict of this kind, we might respond by working harder to please and gain approval, or we may become apologetic and hesitant. Or we might even become defensive and sensitive.

These approaches belong on the list of ways to incubate and escalate conflict. How ironic that our attempts to avoid conflict actually accelerate it!

As uncomfortable as it may be, this is when we need to open the dialogue. What if Sandy had acknowledged the tension and communicated her desire to work more effectively with her boss? At the very least, the conflict would have been exposed to the light and Sandy would have invited a more productive working relationship.

Some conflicts are unspoken; others are outspoken. Let's look at some strategies for turning conflict into collaboration.

Turn Your Objections Into Questions

Here's how that works. If you have a co-worker who is extremely opinionated and overbearing, you may be tempted to give in or push back. There is another option—ask a question. Instead of saying, "This will cost too much," or "We've tried this before and it didn't work," say, "How will we pay for this?" or "How is this different from what we've tried in the past?"

You may experience something just short of a miracle with this strategy. You will find yourself working through even difficult issues more productively.

Another way to deal with very forceful people is to make force unnecessary. Use four of the most powerful words in the English language: "You may be right." Those words being said doesn't mean you think they are right. It just means you are willing to listen to what they have to say.

When you say those words, watch their weapons fall. You can almost see them relax. They were looking for a fight, and they didn't find one. Now you can turn your objections into questions, and another conflict may become collaboration.

Mentally Rehearse Success

Remember Sandy and the dreaded performance review? Sandy did what many of us have done—she mentally rehearsed a disaster.

For days Sandy thought about how terrible this meeting would be. When the appointment finally arrived, she was stretched thin and her emotions were already to the breaking point. It's no wonder she lost control. She had practiced doing that for nearly a week.

Especially when you are going into a difficult situation, mentally rehearse success. How do you want it to turn out? Picture yourself smiling and comfortably working through the issues. Imagine the others involved responding positively.

Seven Simple Ways to Strengthen Your Message Right Now

1. Lose the verbal wince!

One sure sign of passive communication is what I call the verbal wince. This is when you apologize for what you are about to say. It sounds like this:

✓ "I'm not really sure, but I think…"

✓ "I could be wrong, but…"

✓ "This is just my opinion, but…"

You immediately strengthen your communication when you stop wincing!

2. Make eye contact.

This is not a stare down, just comfortable contact. When you fail to meet another's eyes, you look uncomfortable, insecure, or dishonest. Eye contact—or the lack of it—sends an important message.

3. Equalize the posture.

I learned this wonderful lesson from a nurse. She told me when people are sick and hurt in the hospital, they feel small and helpless. There they are lying in a bed or sitting in a wheelchair with people literally standing over them—talking *down at* them. She learned to equalize the posture by pulling up a chair and talking *to* her patients.

This is a simple way to become more assertive immediately. When someone is standing over you, rise to the occasion. When they are sitting, pull up a chair.

4. Memorize a confident posture.

When my son was small and just beginning to play baseball, I learned something wonderful from one of his first coaches. Patiently he stood behind each of the batters, wrapping his hands around theirs on the bat. Over and over, in a slow, deliberate motion, he guided them through the mechanics of a proper swing. He said, "Let your muscles memorize what it feels like to swing the bat correctly."

This is marvelous advice for grown-ups, too. Memorize a confident posture.

What does confidence look like? Confidence stands straight, with shoulders squared, arms relaxed, and the chin up. Confidence does not rock back and forth—as if a baby were sitting on the hip. And it does not fidget with jewelry or locks of hair.

5. Be objective based in your communication.

Go into every communication with a clear objective. This is extremely valuable when the situation is emotionally charged. If you focus on the feelings, they may get the best of you. Focus instead on the objectives—on what you are trying to accomplish.

Another way to be objective based is to choose the right channel of communication. Communication channels are like the stations on your radio. We can communicate by e-mail, voice mail, or in person. Which channel is the best choice? It depends on your objective. If you want to inform or update, perhaps an e-mail or memo is the most efficient way. If you want to change hearts, minds, or behaviors, use the spoken word—preferably with eye contact attached.[7]

An executive summarized this point beautifully when he said, "You're right. We need to type less and talk more around here."

6. Eliminate nonwords and words you use too much.

Nonwords are filler words—words like *uh, um,* and *huh.* We use them to plug the holes of silence, and they weaken our message.

Most of us also have words or phrases we use too often. These are distracting. Listen for those and get rid of them.

7. Align your message for real impact.

Your mother was right. It's not just *what* you say, but *how* you say it that matters, too—it may matter more.

There have been many studies on the impact of words, tone, pace, and body language. Most of them generally agree on these important points:

✓ It's not just words that make a message.

✓ How you say it matters, too.

✓ How you look while you say it matters more.

The visual message is most important for two reasons:

1. It gets there first and sets the stage for everything to follow.

2. If the words and the body don't match, the body will be believed.

That means when we ask how you are, and you say in a clipped, tight-lipped way, "Fine," we don't believe you.

Dress for the Part

Managing the visual message includes our physical presentation. Projecting a professional image doesn't need to be complicated, but it is very important and shouldn't be taken for granted.

In today's work environment the casual code reigns. I'm not convinced this is such a good thing for women. We may want to rethink it.

I've yet to meet a woman who looked more capable in jeans and a T-shirt. And the most successful women I know dress the most professionally. There's a connection here.

When it comes to looking the part, the best advice I ever received was from Marsha Petrie Sue, a very successful speaker. She advised women to "Level it up," or dress one level above the expectation.

That means if you work in a jeans and T-shirt environment, you wear slacks and collared shirts. If slacks are the code, you add a jacket. If jackets are expected, invest in suits. She would also say, "You are not a cow chewing your cud—get rid of the gum." God love her.

Here are some additional tips to consider:

- ✓ Even if you are required to wear a uniform, make sure it is pressed and clean.

- ✓ Avoid hyper-trends, and stick with timeless styles.

- ✓ It's difficult to take a woman with neon-blue, studded talons for nails seriously.

- ✓ When it comes to shoes, take a cue from the gents. Make sure they are polished with no scuffs. Check your heels! If they need repair, fix them or throw them away!

- ✓ Watch the hemline and the neckline! Just because you can wear a miniskirt or a low-cut blouse doesn't mean you should. The women who do are usually the women we work with, not the women we work for. (Go figure.)

- ✓ Pay attention to details like dangling buttons and hems hanging by a thread.

- ✓ If you want to be taken more seriously, dark colors are recommended—flowers, frills, and prints aren't.

- ✓ Jewelry is an accent—not the main attraction.

You can wear whatever you want. You are certainly allowed—encouraged even—to have your own signature and sense of style. Just be aware that your choices create an image, and that image impacts your opportunity—what you are considered for or not considered for.

If you're wondering about the message your appearance is creating, ask for feedback. Go to someone you can trust and ask, "If you didn't know me, what is the first impression you would form based on my appearance?" Then you can decide if changes are necessary.

Send the Invitation

You have a box filled with messages, and now you know how to manage them more effectively—from the inside out. As you implement these ideas, you are inviting people to see you and respond to you in a different way. You are making yourself available for new opportunities and possibilities. You are taking ownership of your communication.

Be patient with yourself as you try new approaches and step out of your comfort zone. Be persistent, too. The change in and around you may be almost imperceptible at first. That is often the case when we grow. Then one day we turn around and find that we are in a new place, and we realize each small step made that possible.

High-Impact Ideas

✓ You have been collecting messages all of your life. Some of them are helping you accomplish marvelous things. Some of them are holding you back.

✓ Communication is the cornerstone of personal effectiveness, and it's an inside-out job.

✓ You are always communicating.

✓ The visual message is important because it arrives first and sets the stage.

✓ What begins as an internal dialogue becomes how we present ourselves to others.

✓ Never say anything to yourself or to anyone else that you do not sincerely wish to be true.

✓ There is a prophet inside you predicting the future.

✓ Working hard and doing exceptional work is not enough. Make your progress visible and your results obvious. Learn to market yourself with authenticity and grace.

✓ Carefully develop the messages—the chapters of your story. Then look for opportunities to tell your story.

✓ Use self-disclosure wisely and purposefully. Consciously choose when and with whom you will make yourself vulnerable.

✓ Turn conflict into collaboration by turning your objections into questions.

✓ Mentally rehearse your success.

✓ Look for ways to strengthen your message.

✓ Your image impacts your opportunity. Dress for the part you want, not the part you have.

Questions for Reflection

Are you facing a difficult encounter at work? Describe that encounter.

_____

_____

_____

What are you rehearsing in the theater of your mind? Take a moment now to rehearse success.

_____

_____

_____

Are you incubating a conflict? Explain.

_____

_____

_____

How can you be more assertive in this situation?

_____

_____

_____

How are you underpresenting yourself or missing opportunities to market yourself?

_____

_____

_____

How effectively do you use self-disclosure?

_____

_____

_____

Action Items

Identify the beliefs that limit you and rewrite those rules.

Keep a log of your self-talk for a week.

Become a collector of signs and phrases. Practice replacing negative frames with positive ones.

Develop your story.

Chapter 3

COMMANDMENT 2:
Empower Yourself—What Are
You Waiting For?

WHEN YOU WERE growing up, did you have a kids' table set up for Thanksgiving dinner? You know, the side table designated for children at holiday dinners. The big table was reserved for grownups. And what a right of passage to finally be invited to sit there!

Many women in the workplace still feel like—or behave as if—they are sitting at the kids' table. We are waiting for an invitation to join the grown-ups.

It may be time for you to pull up your chair and ask for someone to pass the bread!

Right now you may be waiting for someone else to empower you—to give you the things you need to be effective and to feel powerful. And right now I hope you will discover how to empower yourself and how you may be actually giving your power away.

Let's begin with a definition. Empowerment is defined as "equipping or supplying with ability; enabling."

We equip people with tools, information, skills, and confidence. We enable them through training, practice, feedback, support, and encouragement. Others empower us when they give us authority, independence, and even their trust. It's wonderful when that happens. But what if it doesn't?

Then you must look for ways to empower yourself and eliminate what is disempowering. Working from our definition of empowerment, that means you must go get the information, skills, and confidence you need; seek out opportunities to learn and practice; ask for feedback; and build a strong system of encouragement and support.

Shannon leads a customer service team for a large organization. This is a company that is head over heels in love with conference calls, and Shannon spends hours dialed in to these meetings every week. One of the calls she is required to attend is a complete waste of time. The information is either irrelevant or redundant.

Shannon would like to stop attending the call, but she was told she should be there—or it might look bad. So every Wednesday at one o'clock, she is present and accounted for.

I wish Shannon felt free to quit attending the meeting— without feeling guilty—or at the very least, free to offer feedback to make the meeting more productive. I am not suggesting that she defiantly announce she will not be attending these *ridiculous* meetings anymore. I am suggesting that she find a way to protect her time and productivity by professionally confronting anything that steals it.

Shannon is waiting to be excused from the table.

Sabrina also manages a team. Frequently she receives procedure and process updates. She is responsible for covering these changes with her group. After reviewing one of the latest change memos, she has real concerns. She discusses these with her peers, and they don't see a problem. Reluctantly, she implements the changes with her team.

Almost immediately serious problems with the new procedure erupt. Management is thrown into damage-control mode, scrambling to fix the problems created by the change. Service is interrupted and customers are inconvenienced.

When I asked Sabrina why she didn't mention her concerns to her boss, she quietly said, "I didn't want my boss to think I was complaining about the changes, and besides, the other supervisors thought it would be all right. I was the only one who thought there may be a problem."

Sabrina trusted the judgment of others more than she trusted her own—she pushed the "snooze" button on her internal alarm. And she didn't want to appear negative by challenging authority. If she had found a way to do that, a crisis would have been avoided, time would have been saved, and customers would have received the service they expect and deserve.

Sabrina is waiting for permission and consensus.

Cindy supports several attorneys. Each of them is fast paced and results driven, and they rely heavily on her. Her work area is literally surrounded by the attorneys' offices. They rush by tossing assignments and instructions at her: "File this...call him...draft a letter to..." Cindy feels like she is working inside a pinball machine as she is bounced from one priority to another.

What is most disheartening is that none of the attorneys have a full appreciation for what she really does. Each of them only knows what she does for him or her, and all of them believe their work is the top priority. She stays late, comes in early, and frequently works weekends to catch up. Cindy makes it look easy, but it isn't.

Cindy is waiting for someone to realize her workload is out of hand and recognize what it takes to get it all done.

In each of these scenarios, you see hardworking, intelligent women giving their power away. Handing over power may look like:

✓ Waiting for someone to tell you it's OK to recommend a change

✓ Following the group, even when you sense the group should be going in a different direction

✓ Hoping someday, someone will notice how hard you are working

✓ Trusting others' judgment more than your own

Empower Yourself With Options

We back ourselves into cramped corners when we think in terms of yes or no, this or that, do or don't. Always assume there are more options.

This is hard because we are taught to color in the lines. Keep it pretty and don't make a mess. In life and in business sometimes the best answer and the most productive response may be outside the lines.

I love the story about the man who wakes up in the middle of the night soaking wet. Realizing that his waterbed has sprung a leak, he gets up and, half asleep, wrestles the mattress down a flight of stairs and outside. Along the way, the mattress snags on something and rips beyond repair. To make matters worse, it is pouring down rain, and the man slips and falls in the mud. Now he is wet and muddy, sleep deprived, and "mattress-less."

The next day he purchases a new mattress and sets it up. Exhausted from a lack of sleep the night before, he falls gratefully into bed. In the middle of the night he wakes again—soaking wet. It's raining again. This is when he realizes there is a leak in the roof.

Solve the Right Problem

Let's revisit the three scenarios from earlier in this chapter to identify the real problem and look for options "outside the lines."

Shannon's real problem isn't a conference call that wastes her time. Her real problem is that she doesn't feel powerful enough to do anything about it. *Appearances* have become more valuable than productivity. Shannon thinks she has two choices—attend the meeting or don't attend the meeting. What other options exist?

She could partner with co-workers who also attend the meeting. Perhaps they can rotate, each of them taking a turn and taking notes to update the others with a five-minute debriefing or an e-mail. She could provide feedback to make the meeting more valuable. She could ask for guidance. What should she be taking away from this meeting? How should she be using this information?

In Sabrina's situation, the real problem isn't that she didn't speak up more and make a stronger stand. The real problem is *why*. When she looked at this situation, Sabrina saw two clear options. One was to go with the flow and follow instructions. The other option was to be uncooperative and negative. Sabrina wasn't unwilling to speak with the boss about her concerns. But she didn't know how to do that without appearing to be negative. She also didn't want to challenge her boss's authority, and she believed others knew more than she did.

What if Sabrina went to her boss and established some communication ground rules? She might say, "I want to be someone you can count on to do the right things, to support the goals of this department, and to be solutions oriented. When we receive process changes and I have concerns with how those changes will impact our customers, what is the best way for me to communicate that?"

With this approach, Sabrina is not asking permission to confront the issues. She is gaining agreement with her boss on how to confront issues effectively.

Sabrina's case gives us another insight. Everyone—including you—has a *unique* business perspective. By that I mean, you will see things your boss doesn't see. And your perspective is a valuable resource to the organization.

> A consultant was asked to help a grocery store in the Midwest improve customer service. Management may have expected her to come in with a list of improvements and instructions. She didn't. Instead she came with one question, and she asked it of every employee: "What could you personally do to improve the service here?"
>
> Every employee, from management to the most entry-level positions, was asked the same question. Each was expected to come back to the table with at least one idea. One of the answers demonstrates this idea of unique business perspective.
>
> A young woman working in the floral department decided that instead of throwing broken flowers away, she would make corsages and pin them on customers, thanking them for their business. It's a neat idea, isn't it? And it took the employee who throws the flowers away to see it![1]

Empower yourself with the understanding that you will see the business from your vantage point, and you will notice things about the business even your boss doesn't see. Your perspective is valuable, and so is your judgment. Develop that perspective. Trust your judgment. Learn to present your concerns and ideas effectively.

Getting back to our cases, Cindy's real problem isn't how many people she supports or the intense pace of the environment. Her problem is managing expectations and priorities. Cindy needs to make her daily plan more visible to her bosses. She could send a brief e-mail first thing in the morning highlighting the priorities of the day. When new tasks are thrown her way, she could ask for guidance. Pointing to her plan she might say, "I'll be happy to do this for you now. Will you help me reprioritize these tasks?" That is known as "upward delegation," and it is a marvelous way to manage multiple priorities with flexibility.

By the way, when men work on a Saturday, everyone knows. This comes straight from the horse's mouth. Men do not want personal credit for this little tidbit, but the gents are my source. They make a point to call their boss from the office. They don't tell the boss who else is there; they just make sure the boss knows they are there. They also send a periodic e-mail at 2:00 a.m. That doesn't mean they were working all night. They just want you to know they were thinking about work in the middle of the night.

Empower Yourself With Role Clarity

Managers often tell me employees come to them with questions and issues they should be handling independently. When I ask them why they believe employees do this, they give me these reasons:

1. The need for attention

2. The need for reassurance

3. Poor problem-solving and decision-making skills

4. A lack of confidence

5. To avoid responsibility

Nothing on this list is attractive! I've learned from employees there is another reason—it is the lack of role clarity. Employees aren't always sure where their roles and authorities' roles begin and end. We come to our managers for clarification and leave a piece of our credibility behind.

In my consulting practice, I use a very simple tool to empower people through role clarity. This is an informal discussion tool, and

I like it because you can do it on a napkin at lunch. This exercise works. It's called the Roles Box.

If you are a manager, you can use the Roles Box to empower your employees with clarity. If you are an employee, use it to initiate a dialogue with your boss. In both cases, the feedback I receive has been very positive. Here's how it works.

Four quadrants are used to clarify and confirm responsibilities. Begin by listing the things only your manager can do and decide. Next, list the things you can do and decide on your own—without permission or approval.

ROLES BOX	
MANAGER These are the things only the manager can do or decide.	**EMPLOYEE** These are the things the employee does and decides.
RECOMMENDS These are things the manager will ultimately decide based on the employee's recommendation.	**INFORMS** These are the things the employee does while keeping the manager informed.

The Recommends box contains what the manager will ultimately decide, but you can influence the decision with your recommendations. The Informs quadrant is for those things your boss expects you to take care of but needs to be informed of—so he or she is not blindsided if asked for the status.

Once you complete the quadrants, employees and managers should compare notes. You may find gaps in your expectations—that is a good thing. The Roles Box allows you to work through those differences and find clarity.

In one experience with this exercise, a group of three supervisors and their boss—all were women—located significant gaps in perspective and expectation. These gaps were creating serious conflict. The manager was disappointed in what she believed was a lack of initiative and commitment on the part of her supervisory staff. The supervisors felt hesitant and unsupported. This was damaging their confidence in themselves and their leadership.

After completing the Roles Box exercise, there was greater understanding, empowerment, and accountability. Everyone felt better.

Because their roles were evolving, they continued to use the exercise periodically.

As the supervisors gained experience and demonstrated sound judgment, they were given more latitude, authority, and independence. They found that what begins in the Recommends box may move to the Employee quadrant. What is handled exclusively by the Manager may eventually shift to the Recommends quadrant, and so on.

I encourage you to try this exercise. Remember as you grow and demonstrate greater capabilities, expectations will change. You will need to have this conversation more than once.

Initiating the Roles Box conversation prevents you from hesitating when you should take action and from stepping all over someone's feet with too much initiative. There is such thing as too much initiative, and bosses hate it.

What distinguishes positive initiative from the career-limiting kind? I think there are two things. One is motive; the other is wisdom.

It is entirely possible to rush in with the best of intentions and make a big mess. That happens when we don't see the bigger picture and consider the ripple effect of our actions. When we rush to act before thinking about the impact, that's a lack of wisdom and good judgment.

Initiative also backfires when motives are impure. If my actions are self-promoting or self-preserving, it won't look like initiative at all. It will look like political maneuvering or sabotage!

Check your motives, think it through, and demonstrate extreme initiative.

Empower Yourself Through Personal Accountability

In the parable of the talents, three servants are given responsibility.[2] As their master is leaving on a journey, he entrusts each of them with his property—*according to their ability.* One of the servants is given five talents, one receives two talents, and a third is entrusted with a single talent.

It is interesting to note that each of these servants had a different starting position. Some of us start with a lot, and some of us don't. That unfairness is acknowledged in this story and is an excellent metaphor for women in the workplace—our starting position may seem unfair as well.

The point is this: it is not what you start with; it's what you do with it! Two of the servants invested their talents and realized a gain. One dug a hole and buried his talent.

The successful servants in this story were not praised for being profitable. They were recognized for being faithful to what they had been given. The same is true for women at work. We may start with a disadvantage in terms of stereotypes, ceilings of glass, and built-in obstacles, but if we invest our talents wisely, we create a new position.

When the servant who hid his talent was called to account, he blamed the master! We live in a world that encourages and even rewards low accountability. Embracing accountability is empowering, but it may require a complete shift in the way we think about what accountability is.

What comes immediately to mind when you hear, "Who is accountable?"

Did you think of words like *responsibility* or *blame*? Accountability is often associated with blame. That's reasonable. Have you ever seen anyone run through the hallways at the office shouting, "Who's accountable?" when the news is good? I haven't. Normally when we go looking for who's accountable, we aren't measuring them for a medal.

In many organizations, explanations and documentation are

treated like results. In other words, as long as I can explain or document my *lack* of results, I don't really have to have any!

The definition of accountability supports this notion. Look it up! One of the definitions in the dictionary is: "that which can be explained."[3]

| PUBLIC SERVICE ANNOUNCEMENT | *Results and explanations really are different.* |

In their book *The Oz Principle: Getting Results Through Personal and Organizational Accountability,* authors Connor, Smith, and Hickman observe: "Somewhere along the line, society and organizations have stimulated people to feel more responsible for explaining results than for achieving them."[4]

The very moment I decide explanations and results are different, I distinguish myself. I move out of the Zone of Low Accountability and into the victim-free zone. Here I will be taken more seriously, build tremendous credibility, emerge with solutions instead of explanations, and adopt the powerful language of accountability.

The Zone of Low Accountability can be a very attractive place because excuses and explanations can be oh so comforting. We get to say, "It's not my fault," "No one told me," and "That's not my job."

We all go to the Zone of Low Accountability, and reading this book won't change that. It may be natural to go there. You just don't want to set up your tent and stay, because there you are powerless. The key is to quickly recognize when you have entered the zone and get yourself out of there!

It takes courage and resiliency to be accountable. It might mean admitting you have been wrong. Or it may require you to step out of a well-worn comfort zone. Accountability will eventually remind you that your skills are outdated and you need to upgrade. Accountability will cost you something, and it will pay you back in the most extraordinary ways.

Let's look at ways you can embrace and demonstrate personal accountability.

Ask the Right Questions

When bad things happen, our first reaction may be, "Why?" or "Why me?" That may be the most natural response, but it will never be the most productive one.

It is absolutely true: if you ask the wrong question, you will get the wrong answer.

In his book *Flipping the Switch,* John G. Miller gives us some powerful and profound advice: "The answers are in the questions. When we ask better questions, we get better answers.... It's important to remember that these are questions we ask of *ourselves,* not of others."[5]

Have you been to a blame-storming meeting? This is a meeting where we spend the entire time complaining about our situation and blaming something or someone else for it. These meetings frequently happen in the parking lot. People leave a blame-storming meeting exhausted and physically smaller, feeling powerless.

When circumstances are difficult, ask accountable questions. These are questions that redirect energies toward solutions, the future, and options. They sound like:

✓ What can I do?

✓ How am I contributing to the problem?

✓ How do I want this to turn out?

✓ What options are available?

Be a Positive Catalyst!

You can be the most positive catalyst in the workplace. The next time you find yourself trapped in a meeting that has become a whine fest, be the one to step up and ask the accountable question.

When you hear a comment like "When is that department going to get its act together?" be the one to create a shift in thinking. You can ask, "What can we do to partner more effectively with this department?" or "How can we prevent this kind of communication breakdown from happening again?"

How Accountable Are You?

To find your personal accountability score, give yourself a rating of 1, 2, or 3 for each of the following statements:

1—Rarely
2—Sometimes
3—Most of the time

☐ I ask for feedback frequently.

☐ I ask accountable questions of myself.

☐ I focus on things I can do something about and help others do the same.

☐ I own my professional development.

☐ I ask for what I need to be successful.

☐ I fix problems, not blame.

☐ I quickly recognize when I have fallen into the zone of denial, blame, excuses, procrastination, or thinking like a victim.

☐ I step out of my comfort zone and try new approaches to improve my results.

☐ When things don't work, I acknowledge my contribution to the outcome.

☐ When confronted with obstacles, I persevere.

✓ If your score is 24 or higher, congratulations! You are empowering yourself with accountable behaviors.

✓ If you scored 18 or higher, you are demonstrating accountability with room to grow. You can empower yourself even more. You can be more of a positive catalyst.

✓ If your score is below 18, personal accountability is an area needing real focus. This is good news! You have found an important key to empowerment.

Regardless of your score, I encourage you to choose three areas for personal focus. Test yourself again in thirty days to measure your progress.

Empower Yourself Through Optimism

Negativity in the workplace is an absolute epidemic. Managers and employees alike struggle against what feels like an ever-increasing tide of negativity; it literally weakens a body, a career, a team, and ultimately the organization.

Workplace negativity has many sources. They include:

✓ Poor leadership

✓ Lack of recognition

✓ Rapid, disconnected change

✓ Limited resources

✓ Nonperforming co-workers

✓ Constant pressure to do more with less

✓ Fear and uncertainty

✓ Poor communication

Even this short list is enough to depress anyone!

Studies confirm that the most successful lives, careers, and companies are marked by a relentless optimism. The most successful CEOs are optimistic about the future. Even in the most challenging times, they never lose sight of their vision. Studies have even shown that optimistic workers increase their opportunities for advancement and have the potential to earn more.[6] Optimistic people present themselves with more confidence. They believe in their ability to overcome obstacles and achieve the goal. They are resilient and look to the future with expectancy.

The book *Good to Great* by Jim Collins is an extensive study on how a good company can become a great one. A common attribute of great organizations was "...the unwavering faith that [they would] prevail."[7] Collins found an unrelenting optimism in these great companies.

The difference between an optimist and a pessimist is the way they think about, talk about, and respond to setbacks.

We all have an explanation style—it's the way we interpret life events. In his book *Learned Optimism,* Dr. Martin Seligman presents the explanatory style as a habit of thinking.[8] Negativity is simply unchecked pessimism.

Your explanation is the sum of four factors: duration, orientation, responsibility, and scope. These four elements create DORS. And with every event, you will step through one of two DORS.

- ✓ *Duration* speaks to how long you think the event will last. For a pessimist, it will be forever! "This will *never* change. It will *always* be this way. We will *never* be the same." An optimist sees the same event differently. For the optimist, it is a temporary setback.

- ✓ *Orientation* is the direction you are looking. Pessimists look backward. They talk about what happened or didn't happen—what should have or shouldn't have occurred. Optimists look to the future. They talk about what needs to happen or what happens next.

✓ *Responsibility* reveals your focus or intention. Pessimists need to blame: "It's all your fault." "It's all my fault." The point is that someone must be blamed—and preferably punished. Optimists are not interested in blame. Their focus is on the solution. They want to fix the problem, not the blame.

✓ *Scope* tells us how much is impacted by this event. How big is this situation? Pessimists will tell you it is huge: "*Everything* is ruined. *Everyone* is upset. *Nothing* is working the way it should." Optimists isolate issues. They say, "This is a problem," or "This isn't working the way it should."

Let's look at how the same situation looks very different depending on the style of explanation.

Judy and Carol work for an organization that has recently reorganized. Both of them are now reporting to new bosses, and their roles have changed considerably. Judy is struggling to accept the changes. She explains recent events this way:

"I used to love working here. This was a great company, and I can remember when we were like one big family. Everything has changed, and we'll never be like that again. Management just doesn't care, and everyone is so unhappy now."

Carol has a different report. She is working through the same change, but her interpretation is one of hope.

"We have seen a lot of change, and some of it has been difficult. In the next couple of weeks, things will settle down and we'll find our equilibrium. The important thing right now is to remain flexible. I am sure there will be rough spots along the way, but we'll take those bumps one at a time. The company has grown. That's a testament to our success, and it brings new challenges and new opportunities."

As the examples above so clearly illustrate, the explanation style is important, because how you explain an event determines how you respond to it. Read those two explanations again. Which one sounds like leadership? Which one sounds more credible?

Optimism is a predictor of success for two reasons.

1. Those who learn this skill see themselves overcoming obstacles and crossing the finish line.

2. Those who see this skill in you see glimpses of leadership.

Responding to Negativity in Others

While you are working to practice optimism, there is a force working against you. Unfortunately, negativity is more natural—you don't have work at it—and true optimism is rare.

Negativity catches. I wish we could get an annual negativity shot to immunize ourselves against what is negative, toxic, and unproductive at work.

If you are serious about empowering yourself, breaking negative thought patterns, and learning optimism, you must be prepared to deal with negativity in others. This can be very hard for women because we are nurturing. We don't want to hurt anyone's feelings, we don't want to be rude, and we don't know how to tell this negative person they are sucking the life right out of us! So we listen and try to be supportive.

What begins as a shoulder to lean on and a listening ear can become very toxic. Before long we find ourselves knee-deep in the muck and drowning in the same attitude we tried to rescue.

You may work with someone right now who wants to whine and complain constantly. There are two reasons you need to stop this now. The first is guilt by association. Like it or not, your reputation and your credibility are damaged when you associate with negative people at work. We all need to take Jack Canfield's advice, "Avoid toxic people!"[9]

The second reason to take immediate action is the impact negativity has on your attitude and your productivity. It is impossible to spend your lunch hour complaining about your job, your boss, or your customers and then return to work energized and dynamic! Instead you schlep back to work carrying the weight of the world on your shoulders. You'll be schlepping and slumping all the way back to your desk.

How do you shut off the tap of negativity and make yourself unavailable for that kind of communication? There are steps you can take to gracefully and firmly stop the negative flow.

1. Acknowledge what this person is feeling. It's OK to say, "I know you're very disappointed or discouraged."

2. Create a future focus: "How do you want this to turn out?" or "What needs to happen for you to feel better about this situation?"

3. Transition a conversation about problems to a conversation about solutions: "What can you do to improve the outcome? What are you willing to try?"

4. Offer options and alternatives: "What if you were to...?" One of two things is going to happen. Either you will help someone who is stuck in a negative pattern, or this person won't come to you anymore. Either of these outcomes is perfectly OK with me. Some people don't want to be unstuck. They like sticking, and they want you to stick with them. My motto is: either fix it or forget it.

If you implement these steps and still find yourself ambushed by negativity, you may need to become more direct. That conversation sounds like, "I want to help find solutions. Let's agree to talk about what you can do to make it better—what you personally control.

That will empower you to make the necessary changes."

Chances are pretty slim that the negative people will actually read this. When I speak on negativity in the workplace, the negative people don't come—unless they are dragged! It's the people trying to deal with the negative people who actually show up. Just in case, if you are the negative person, please stop! Your negativity is draining, and the people who are trying to support you are tired of holding you up.

Empower Yourself With Ground Rules

When communication becomes unproductive or conflicts arise, it is often because there are no established rules of engagement or ground rules in place.

Ground rules are operating agreements. These are prearranged decisions about how you do business—how you handle conflict, manage sensitive or confidential information, and communicate. I encourage you to set boundaries and protect your credibility with a personal set of operating agreements.

Here are a few examples of communication ground rules that foster loyalty, build trust, and empower you.

1. I am loyal to the person who isn't in the room.[10]

2. I speak to issues, not about them—to people, not about them.

3. I talk about what I can impact.

4. My conversations are solutions oriented.

5. I am committed to productive communication, and I ask for the same in return.

Ground rules are good guides. They keep you on track. They are also good teachers. When someone comes to you with the latest juicy gossip about Susie in accounts payable, you simply say, "Wait! I have this communication rule about being loyal to the person who isn't in the room. I want to hear every juicy detail of your story. Please wait here while I go get her!"

The gossip won't be there when you return, and she won't bring you her communication trash again.

When you consider the stereotypes already in place—you know the notions about women being catty, gossipy, and dependent—ground rules aren't an option. Without them we risk falling right into those roles and reinforcing those assumptions!

You Do Have Choices

In every situation, you have three choices. You may not always like them, but you have exactly three.

1. *You can choose to accept the situation for what it is and how it is.* Acceptance means no more talking about it, worrying over it, or giving your strength to it. At this point you may be thinking, "No way, sister. My situation is completely unacceptable." That's all right. You have two choices left.

2. *You can work to change it.* You can seek a new perspective and try a new approach. Now you may be thinking, "I did that. I have exhausted myself with it. I've tried everything. Nothing worked." No worries, you still have another choice.

3. *You can leave it.* Now you may be thinking, "What! That's ridiculous. I can't leave my job. I have to work for a living." No, actually you don't. A lot of people don't work for a living—they give up some stuff, like food and electricity, but working for a living is entirely optional. Even so, you may not want to leave it. That's OK, too. But if you choose not to leave it, you must return to option 1 or option 2.

The tragedy is living or working as if you don't have a choice. You do have choices. You have exactly *three*.

High-Impact Ideas

✓ We cannot wait for others to equip and enable us for success. Ultimately it is our responsibility to empower ourselves. That means we need to go get the information, skills, and confidence we need. We must search out opportunities to learn and practice new skills. It's our job to ask for feedback and build a strong system of encouragement and support.

✓ We back ourselves into cramped corners when we think in terms of yes or no, this or that, do or don't. Always assume there are more options available.

✓ Solve the right problem. Quite often the surface issue is just a symptom. Look below the symptom to find the real problem.

✓ There is an expectation gap between managers and employees. If unmanaged, this gap creates disappointment and conflict. Eliminate the gap by clarifying roles.

✓ Your starting position may be unfair. Where you begin is not the point. Invest your talents wisely to create a new position.

✓ Explanations and results really are different.

✓ When your circumstances are challenging, ask accountable questions—questions that point you and others to solutions, the future, and options.

✓ Be the positive catalyst at work.

✓ We all have an explanation style, a way we interpret life events—what we think and say about an event, how we explain it. Your explanation style is the sum of four factors: duration, orientation, responsibility, and scope. These four elements create DORS, and with every event you will step through one of two DORS.

✓ Optimism is a predictor of success. Those who learn this skill see themselves overcoming obstacles and crossing the finish line. Those who see this skill in you see glimpses of leadership.

✓ Immunize yourself from negativity. Avoid toxic people!

✓ Establish personal ground rules to protect your credibility, build trust, and foster loyalty.

✓ In every situation, you have three choices—accept, change, or leave it. Believing or behaving as if you have no choices is a tragedy.

Questions for Reflection

In what ways might you be hiding your talents?

_____

_____

_____

How might you be trying to solve the wrong problem?

_____

_____

_____

Which situation could be transformed by asking the right questions?

_____

_____

_____

What is your explanation style?

_____

_____

_____

What DORS are you walking through?

_____

_____

_____

How are you giving your power away by behaving or believing you have no choice?

_____

_____

_____

Action Items

Use one of your challenging situations as a case study. Consider the options you might find outside the lines.

Develop an explanation style that empowers you to clear the hurdles and achieve results. When you are faced with a difficult circumstance, practice using the DORS model.

Develop your personal ground rules for communication.

Chapter 4

COMMANDMENT 3:
Equip Yourself With Awareness

AWARENESS IS ESSENTIAL to surviving and thriving. This has always been true, and never more so than in today's workplace. The rules and expectations are changing. There is constant pressure to do more with less. Competition is fierce, and the race to innovation is accelerating. The challenge is enormous. The opportunity is amazing.

Do an Internet search on the word *awareness*, and you'll find hundreds of awareness campaigns. These causes promote early detection, prevention, and understanding. That's very appropriate for your cause as well. For women in the workplace, awareness is a key concept.

At the cornerstone of awareness are the emotional intelligence (EI) competencies. We call them competencies because they can be learned. That's exciting because these competencies account for greater percentages of success in every field.

In the workplace there is often a focus—sometimes even an arrogance—around technical competencies. Technical skills are certainly important, but we are beginning to understand those skills don't stand well alone. We've all met people who are highly educated and very intelligent, but they can't communicate their way out of a paper bag! All of that knowledge and intelligence is mute if we can't connect with people in a meaningful way.

So the scorecards are in, and people with high emotional intelligence win. Emotional intelligence gives IQ impact. It determines the level of relationship, and relationship determines the level of result.

What Is Emotional Intelligence?

Emotional intelligence is a set of intuitive skills. You may not even be aware when you are using them. These skills include confidence, perseverance, empathy, enthusiasm, and self-motivation. If you can make these a more conscious choice, you give yourself more control. In that way, emotional intelligence is awareness. Increase your EI by increasing your awareness on many levels.

In the book *The EQ Difference,* Adele B. Lynn calls emotional intelligence your "inner bird dog."[1] People with high emotional intelligence have internalized a set of skills allowing them to be centered and poised even in the most difficult situations. We are drawn to people with high emotional intelligence. We are attracted to their confidence and how we feel when we are with them. We connect with these people because they understand us. These people read situations differently. They see things others don't—intuitively understanding what others miss.

People with high emotional intelligence:[2]

- ✓ *Recognize what they are feeling and why.* They understand the impact of their emotions on relationships and results.

- ✓ *Assess themselves accurately.* They are aware of their strengths and weaknesses. They seek feedback and use it to grow.

- ✓ *Are confident and self-assured.* They are decisive and can stand alone if necessary.

✓ *Demonstrate focus and self-control.* They manage impulses and remain composed even in difficult, stressful situations.

✓ *Build trust*—through authenticity and integrity.

✓ *Take responsibility.* They hold themselves accountable.

✓ *Adapt.* They flex with multiple demands, change, and shifting priorities.

✓ *Innovate.* They are open to new approaches and ideas; they seek fresh perspectives.

✓ *Are self-motivated.* These are results-oriented people with a strong drive for performance and excellence.

✓ *Are deeply committed* to the goals of the group or organization.

✓ *Take extreme initiative.* They exceed expectations.

✓ *Operate from an optimistic frame.* They persist in the face of adversity and setbacks.

✓ *Empathize with others*—listen between the words.

✓ *Have a service orientation.* They know how to meet customers' needs and create loyalty.

✓ *Develop and encourage others*—through recognition, feedback, and challenge.

✓ *See diversity as an opportunity* to leverage different backgrounds and perspectives.

✓ *Understand the politics*—the social networks and forces that shape perspectives and behaviors.

✓ *Influence others.* They are persuasive—able to build consensus and support.

✓ *Communicate effectively.* They give and receive information well. They reach for a deeper understanding and create open dialogue.

✓ *Inspire people* with a compelling vision.

✓ *Initiate change* and challenge the status quo.

✓ *Manage conflict and negotiate effectively.* They design win-win outcomes.

✓ *Build a network of strong relationships.*

✓ *Invite collaboration* and work with others to achieve shared goals.

✓ *Create team performance and identity.*

Before reading on, review the list again. With this description in mind, who is your emotional intelligence role model? Who in your life or work embodies these attributes and skills? How many of these statements describe you? Which ones do you need to work on?

Where Do Your Emotions Take You?

Emotions begin as feelings—anger, happiness, fear, and so on. When we express our feelings, they translate into behaviors. Those behaviors create results. Unless monitored with awareness and self-control, our emotions can actually drive us away from the results we want to achieve.

To better understand the link between emotions, behavior, and performance, try this exercise:

1. Think of the best boss you've ever had. What made this boss so effective?

2. Now think of the worst boss you've worked for. What made this boss so ineffective?

3. How did you feel working for each of these people?

4. What did you do? What behaviors did these feelings evoke?

MY BEST BOSS...	HOW I FELT...	WHAT I DID...
Encouraged me to take risks. Recognized me. Allowed me to learn from my mistakes. Cared about me as person.	Confident Appreciated Safe to learn Valuable	Stepped out of my comfort zones. Worked harder. Took responsibility and learned from my mistakes. Demonstrated loyalty.

MY WORST BOSS...	HOW I FELT...	WHAT I DID...
Took credit for my ideas. Criticized me in public. Played favorites. Ignored me.	Unmotivated Humiliated Angry Unvalued	Stopped sharing my ideas. Defended myself and blamed others. Withdrew from the team. Stopped caring.

These tables illustrate the direct connection between *how we feel* and *what we do*. It's easy to see how feelings inspire responses. In a negative cycle our feelings can actually drive us away from what we want and need.

More than once Anita's boss has taken credit for her ideas, and this infuriates her. She stops offering solutions and even allows a problem to escalate out of control—a problem she could have easily solved if she hadn't been determined to punish her boss. As a result, her department and her boss looked unprepared and incompetent. Mission accomplished.

In this example, Anita's emotional response has taken her further from her goal. She needed credit for her work. She forfeited that recognition and lost credibility!

Emotional Intelligence Begins With Self-Awareness

The best news about emotional intelligence is that you can have more. In fact you can have as much as you want. The only catch is to have more EI, you must have more awareness, and that begins with self.

The first goal is to be more aware of our responses, reactions, and needs. As this awareness grows, we are able to develop objective-based responses.

On their own, emotions make terrible drivers, bad guides, and worse decision makers. Emotions will hijack you if you let them. They will pick you up and carry you off! When the ride is over, you may find yourself further from your goals and intentions. I have learned it is a long walk home.

This can be a huge problem for women in the workplace. We are already labeled as emotional, needy, and irrational. When we allow emotions to drive the car, we perpetuate the stereotypes.

In the previous example, Anita allowed negative feelings to drive, and they took her even further from the recognition she wanted. What would an objective-based response have looked like?

If her objective is to be credited for her ideas and solutions, she may need to find new approaches for presenting her ideas and marketing her results. She may need to talk about her results in a different way and find appropriate opportunities to market her efforts internally—without throwing her boss under the bus. She might say, "I really enjoyed working on this project. The most rewarding part was working through the challenge of..."

Perhaps getting credit isn't the real issue for Anita. The larger problem here is weak leadership. To succeed, Anita will have to learn how to manage her manager. She must consciously rein in the emotions and learn to ask a new set of questions:

✓ How am I feeling?

✓ Why am I feeling that way?

✓ What do I need?

✓ What am I afraid will happen?

✓ How do I want this to turn out?

✓ What can I do to achieve the result I need?

The moment you begin this self-inquiry, a switch flips in your brain. You are moving from a purely emotional response to an objective-based response.

Instead of being packed off by our emotions, we can teach objectives to drive. We can learn to ask new questions of ourselves, to tell ourselves the truth, and take conscious, deliberate steps in the direction of our goal.

Go Get Your Feedback!

Self-awareness comes from other sources as well. If we allow it, feedback can be a marvelous tool. A dear colleague and friend of mine sometimes says, "Feedback is a gift, and boy, do I have a present for you!"

Feedback is all around you. It is in what people say or don't say. It is in facial expressions and body language. It's in the cooperation or resistance you encounter. There is feedback in the way your ideas are received and the questions you are asked.

Emotional intelligence is marked by accurate self-assessment—knowing one's strengths and weaknesses. Have you met someone who is painfully unaware of how badly they come across to others—demanding, defensive, argumentative, or inappropriate? What is the cost of this low awareness? How much time and energy do they spend overcoming the resistance of their own making? How much are their relationships damaged? What opportunities do they forfeit?

Yes, feedback is a gift, and for most employees the package arrives once or twice a year. It is the much anticipated performance evaluation.

When you stop and think about it, it is just ludicrous to sit back and passively wait for another person to tell you how you are performing at work. The reality is most employees do. The performance is yours, and so is the feedback. You own it. Go get it!

Instead of waiting for the performance review—that most employees dread more than extensive dental work—initiate a dialogue. Ask for feedback.

Your goal is to highlight accomplishments, agree on areas needing more focus, discuss action items, and determine how you will mark progress. Here are some questions you can use to get the conversation moving:

- ✓ What do you see as my greatest strengths?

- ✓ Where would you like to see greater effort?

- ✓ What skills do I need to be more effective?

- ✓ Where do you wish I would spend more time? Less time?

- ✓ How can I have a more positive impact here?

- ✓ How can I become more valuable to this organization?

Questions like this are not for the fainthearted, but they are irresistible! Imagine someone asking these questions of you. What impression would you have of a person who is this interested in being the best they can possibly be?

When I ask managers what they would think of an employee who calls a meeting to initiate this kind of conversation, I hear a unanimous, "Wow!" Most managers then say this has never, ever happened to them.

Several positive things are triggered when you have the courage to ask for feedback. It's disarming and solutions based. If there is tension or you sense there's a problem, asking for feedback allows you to isolate the issues so you can do something about them. You demonstrate maturity and personal accountability. You called the meeting, so you get to drive the agenda! And above all, it immediately sets you apart from everyone who isn't proactively managing their feedback.

Get ready. Hang on. You will hear some things you don't like—things you don't agree with. You may be tempted to argue about your feedback or explain yourself. *Resist that temptation with all of your might!*

When you receive feedback, simply say, "Thank you."

That doesn't mean you agree with everything that has been said. It simply means you appreciate the honesty. Later you can decide how to use the feedback or, if you disagree, how to manage the perception you have discovered.

As you search for feedback, keep it in perspective. The feedback you receive isn't necessarily *who you are.* It doesn't define or limit you. It is a perception. In order to manage perceptions, you must understand what they are and how they are created.

Amanda is young and aggressive. She has been identified as high potential and participates in the organization's mentoring program. She is opinionated and outspoken. Unfortunately, most of her contributions are negative. She argues insignificant points and regularly positions herself on the opposite side of discussions.

Honestly? She wears me out, and I told her so.

She was shocked to learn that I found her to be distracting and counterproductive. She thought of herself as edgy and thought provoking—an independent thinker, challenging the status quo.

I encouraged Amanda not to take my word for it. After all, mine is just one perception. I challenged her to closely monitor the reactions and responses of her colleagues, gather additional feedback, and decide for herself if changes were warranted.

About a month later I saw Amanda again. The transformation was incredible! She was still outspoken, but in a productive way. When I congratulated her on the adjustment she had obviously made, she had a confession to make.

She said, "When you gave me the feedback, I was very angry—first with you and later with myself. I pouted for a few days. I decided to punish everyone by not saying anything at all. When I finally came around, I realized I wasn't having the impact I want to have on this group. I want to be known for initiating change, not conflict. I've asked a few of my colleagues to give me feedback on the adjustments I'm making, and I notice people responding to my ideas more positively."

I love the honesty in that! Amanda received difficult feedback. She processed the data emotionally for a minute, and then she used the feedback to make positive changes. When she asked her peers to help monitor her progress, she took the feedback to a whole new level. She owned it.

If you take charge of your feedback, you'll never need to dread another performance review. There will be no surprises. Your evaluation will simply summarize the conversations you have initiated throughout the year.

Go get your gift and open it early!

Increase Your Awareness of Others

On the next level, we become more aware of others. This awareness of others allows us to leverage diversity as a distinct set of relationship skills. We reach for a deeper understanding, challenging our perceptions and assumptions. We learn how to bring the best out in others.

One of my dearest friends and a member of my "extended family" is a master at bringing out the best in others. She looks below the behavior to find what is driving it. She reaches beneath what is unattractive—even obnoxious—to find a glimpse of good. Then she focuses on that goodness. The amazing thing is how people respond to her. By focusing on what is good in people, she brings it to the surface!

Our awareness of others—our ability to understand and connect in a meaningful way—is constrained by preconceived notions, assumptions, perceptions, and labels.

Check the Labels

We all label people. It is our way of organizing, arranging, and categorizing. We put stuff—even people—in neat little boxes with labels attached to remind us what's inside. What is worse than the labels we slap on people is the behavior it evokes.

Labels become filters that we listen through, and they can actually reinforce themselves. This is a bit like chickens and eggs. Which came first, the label or the behavior?

Let's say I work with you, and I have labeled you as "defensive." I need to speak with you about something today. It's not a big deal, but you will make it a big deal—because that's what defensive people do.

As I approach you, I am ready for a defensive response. My posture is tense and rigid. My father used to call this stance "loaded for bear."

What does that look like to you? An attack! You see me coming—loaded for bear—and you prepare to defend yourself. We have our encounter, and it does become argumentative and confrontational. I walk away, shaking my head, saying to myself how defensive and obnoxious you are.

What just happened? First I labeled you. Then I reached into the situation, pulled out a defensive response, and judged you for it! How convenient is that?

Years ago while traveling in England, I ran across a book called *Miller's Bolt* by Thomas Stirr.[3] It is a wonderful book—a business parable—about building and rebuilding professional relationships. Inside the story is an exercise that I found fascinating and rewarding. I'd like to share it with you.

Think of someone you have a difficult time communicating with and relating to. This is someone you need to communicate with frequently and a relationship you care about. If you don't care about the person or the relationship, skip this exercise. It won't work.

Once you have this person in mind, write down three words describing them. Chances are the words that come immediately to mind won't be a glowing report.

The words you have written down are the labels you have virtually pasted to the forehead of this difficult person. This is the box you have put them in. Every communication must pass through this filter; you are actually responding to the label, not the person.

For the communication to change, the filter must change. You must reach for a deeper understanding. Do that by neutralizing the negative filter.

In some cases it's easy to neutralize or even find a positive aspect to the label. "Picky" might become "detail oriented." "Pushy" in a more positive frame could be "direct." Sometimes it is harder to reframe the behavior.

Let's say I am having trouble with my boss; I describe her as a "control freak." How do I neutralize that? I may need to reach below the behavior to the cause. What causes a person to over control? It is fear. My boss is afraid. When I remove the "control freak" label and replace it with "afraid," something marvelous happens. I will respond differently to someone who is afraid.

I have released you from the box and allowed for a new pattern of communication.

One of the demonstrations I frequently use in leadership workshops is uncanny—almost frightening actually. I select five participants from the audience and ask them to step up to the front of the room. Here, five chairs are arranged.

I place a hat on each volunteer. On each hat is a label. One of the volunteers is labeled a leader. Others are labeled negative, people-pleaser, and lazy. The last volunteer is labeled invisible. The volunteers can see the labels on each other, but they do not know what their own label is.

They are told they have been chosen to serve on a special employee committee. This goal of this group is to recommend ways to improve employee motivation and morale. They are instructed to meet now for ten minutes to discuss ideas and draft a plan. The only rule is they must respond to the labels of their colleagues.

No matter what is said, they are to use the labels to formulate their response. I then turn to the volunteer labeled as leader and ask this person to lead the meeting. She looks a little surprised initially, but she quickly steps into the role. Each time the leader speaks, the room agrees. We hang on every word. The other volunteers direct their comments and ideas to the leader. Within minutes the leader is sitting taller and taking charge. She is acting like a leader. Why? Because she is being treated like one!

Remember the invisible volunteer? Each time she speaks, she is ignored. She is interrupted and her ideas are discounted. Very quickly she shuts down. She says nothing and stares at the floor. She has indeed become invisible.

This exercise teaches us that we can bring out the best or the worst in others. People with high EI purposefully and deliberately bring out the best.

The exercise also reminds us that we are all carrying labels—like those name tags they slap on you at conferences. While we don't always know what the labels say, they are inspiring responses from others. They are the context for communication.

Reach for a Deeper Understanding

In *The Seven Habits of Highly Effective People,* Dr. Stephen Covey teaches, "Seek first to understand, then to be understood."[4] This is a ground rule for empathy.

Empathy is simply the willingness to try to understand how another feels. It is not agreement. It is reaching for a deeper understanding.

I learned about empathy from a young woman at the Dallas/ Fort Worth International Airport. I was making a connection on my way to Boston when a huge thunderstorm brought everything to a grinding halt. Connections were lost, and the travel nightmare began. Situations like this do not bring the best out in people.

I found myself in the dreaded customer service line. This, by the way, is an oxymoron. There should be no line in customer service. This long line was weaving through the concourse, and the people in it were grumpy. They were taking their frustrations out on the young woman behind the counter. She, on the other hand, was doing a marvelous job of provoking everyone—she was horrible really.

I do believe in objective-based communication and immediately found my objective. I was going to make her cry. It was a public service really.

With that goal in mind I began preparing my speech, and it was coming together beautifully. When my turn finally came, I stepped up to the counter ready to unleash the lecture guaranteed to put this rude woman in her place. That is when I remembered the real goal. Get to Boston. I had wasted my waiting time preparing for the wrong objective!

In that split second the only thing I could think of was to empathize. So I did. I said to her, "I cannot imagine how it must feel to stand behind that counter with a hundred people waiting to yell at me." She burst into tears. It was one of the finest moments of my life.

Then she taught me something I will never forget. She said, "I don't control the weather. I don't control when the planes come or when they go. I do control who sits on them and where. In situations like this, I try to save a seat in first class for the person who is kind."

I sat in that seat—4B, to be exact.

I learned empathy is powerful. It quite literally gets you where you need to go. And that's not the end of my lesson. When I began to try to understand how she might be feeling behind that counter, I didn't see a rude gate agent. I saw a young woman without the skills, tools, or support she needed to deal with the situation she was in. I still did not agree with her behavior, but I could understand it. I could even relate to it. I've been there.

When I stood in judgment of her, she was the enemy. Empathy opened a door of understanding and created a whole new possibility—and a seat in first class.

Develop a Sense for the Situation

When we step into the level of developing a sense for a particular situation, we are in the moment and keenly aware of the circumstances. We understand the undercurrents, hidden agendas, and sensitivities. We read between the lines and hear what isn't said. And we think about the stakeholders and the stakes—understanding what people have, or perceive, to gain or to lose.

Consider Chris, who was asked by her boss to review a set of procedures and make recommendations to improve them. This was right up her alley—a definite strength. She set about evaluating the procedures and found them cumbersome and redundant.

In a staff meeting, she mentioned her work on the procedures and let the group know how much easier the new process would be for them. Chris thought she was bringing good news to her hardworking colleagues, and she expected them to be relieved and grateful.

An awkward silence filled the room. Chris didn't realize the original authors of the procedure were sitting in that meeting. To them, her good news was like cold water in the face.

Situational awareness protects us from stepping in something or stomping on toes. Think of it like the ridges on the sides of a freeway lane. If you run over those, you certainly know it. They alert you—you've edged out of your lane. Correct your course!

Understand Your Organization

Organizations are a collection of beliefs and values and norms. With each organization there are a set of rules—what is acceptable and what is not. Some of the rules are unspoken, and some of the boundaries are like a trip wire—you don't see them until you've already stumbled.

A client shared this example of how painful low organizational awareness can be.

> Not long after joining the human resources team for a global organization, Deborah embarked on several exciting initiatives. She was developing new tools and processes for performance appraisals, and she worked tirelessly for months to deliver a state-of-the-art system.
>
> It was good work—great work actually. She was bringing her organization out of the dark ages and into the light!
>
> When Deborah began to implement the changes, she felt some resistance. It was nothing dramatic, just a little push back. She began to wonder if this was too much, too soon, from someone too new. Perhaps smaller steps would be more welcome and more effective.
>
> Deborah's boss encouraged her to forge ahead: "Push on, sister, push on!" So she did. That's when the rug was pulled out from under her.

There was so much resistance to the new program coming from a new person—who does this girl think she is anyway?—in what had always been a very male-dominated company. The program was swiftly pulled from the agenda.

If that weren't demoralizing enough, this boss—who had encouraged Deborah to push on—was suddenly very quiet on the topic. She found herself standing quite alone in the project wreckage.

My client learned several things she will never forget:

1. Before you build things for an organization, you have to build credibility inside of it.

2. Organizations do have "secret codes." If you don't have the combination, you will be locked out.

3. Nothing replaces leadership inside of change.

When I asked Deborah what she would have done differently, she said, "I would build trust and involve people in the proposed changes more. I would identify key players throughout the organization to endorse the new process. I would trust my intuition. Instead of trying to plow through the resistance, I would work to understand and remove it."

I am happy to report that Deborah is now successfully implementing powerful and positive initiatives within her organization. She has developed a deep understanding of how the organization works, and she has cultivated the credibility, influence, and relationships to get real traction.

Anticipatory Awareness

Anticipatory awareness is readiness. Readiness is difficult because it is easy to become very task oriented in our work—to lose sight of the big picture. We develop anticipatory awareness or readiness by continually asking, "What's next?"

Columnist George F. Will once wrote, "The future has a way of arriving unannounced." Many organizations are being forced to reinvent themselves. They must change or face extinction. This ability to change is the combination of two factors—awareness and ability. When you add those pieces together, you get change-ability. To grow and thrive in the future, organizations—and the people in them—must increase their change-ability.

When faced with the realization that the future has arrived, and they weren't ready for it, clients often say, "Why didn't we see this coming?" The answer is simple: "We weren't searching for it. We didn't ask the right questions. We let ourselves get comfortable."

I like the advice from Jack Welch when he said, "Change before you have to."

Incidentally, whether you are on the front line or in management, anticipatory awareness is an essential skill. This kind of thinking isn't reserved for ivory towers, boardrooms, and executive retreats. The moment you begin thinking like this you become more valuable to the organization.

Read business journals and study successful people. Develop super-sensitive change radar. Practice anticipatory thinking by asking questions like:

✓ What questions should we have been asking ourselves five years ago?

✓ What will our customers need/expect in five years?

✓ How will my position or the skills required of me be different in the future?

✓ What will drive our competitive advantage?

✓ What will be our greatest challenges—internally and externally?

Problems and challenges are excellent change detectors. These are red flags waving in the wind, telling you something must change!

Just like communication, awareness is also an inside-out job. It starts with self-awareness and ultimately becomes our connection with the future. These emotional intelligence skills give us more control and credibility—they become keys that unlock our possibilities.

High-Impact Ideas

✓ Emotional intelligence gives IQ impact. It determines the level of relationship, and relationship determines the level of result.

✓ In the simplest terms, emotional intelligence is awareness. You increase your EI by increasing your awareness on many levels.

✓ When we express our feelings, they translate into behaviors. Those behaviors create results. Unless monitored with self-control and awareness, our emotions can actually drive us away from the results we want to achieve.

✓ "Check in" with yourself frequently to ask for what you need and avoid "emotional hijacking."

✓ Feedback is all around you. It is in what people say or don't say. It is in facial expressions and body language. It is in the cooperation or resistance you encounter. There is feedback in the way your ideas are received and the questions you are asked. Take charge of your feedback.

✓ Our awareness of others—our ability to understand and connect in a meaningful way—is constrained by preconceived notions, assumptions, perceptions, and labels.

✓ Labels become filters. Every communication passes through this filter; you are actually responding to the label, not the person. For the communication to change, the filter must change. You must reach for a deeper understanding. Do that by neutralizing the negative filter.

✓ Empathy is simply the willingness to try to understand how another feels. It is not agreement. It is reaching for a deeper understanding.

✓ Before you build things for an organization, you have to build credibility inside of it.

✓ Organizations do have secret codes. If you don't have the combination, you will be locked out.

✓ Nothing replaces leadership inside of change.

✓ Develop super-sensitive change radar. Anticipate the future and keep asking, "What's next?"

Questions for Reflection

Which is driving your future, emotions or objectives?

_____

_____

_____

What labels are you assigning?

_____

_____

_____

Which labels are you wearing?

_____

_____

_____

How can you help your organization prepare for the future?

_____

_____

_____

Action Items

Search for EI role models—people with high emotional intelligence. Observe their approaches and responses. How are they different and more successful than others who may be in the same situation? Look for the intuitive skills they use.

Cue yourself to "check in" at least three times a day. What are you feeling? Why are you feeling that way? What do you need?

Check your labels. For the next week pay close attention to the labels you have attached to people and how those labels are influencing your interactions. Notice how positive labels inspire productive communication and negative labels limit the relationship. Consciously neutralize negative labels and monitor the change in communication.

Make an appointment with your boss to ask for feedback.

Chapter 5

COMMANDMENT 4:
Become a Skilled Negotiator

REPEAT AFTER ME, "Everything is negotiable, and I can be a great negotiator!"

Let's play a negotiation game. The rules are simple. Begin with question 1 and let your answers guide you to the next step.

1. Are you paid enough for what you do?	If your answer is no, proceed to question 2. If your answer is yes, the game is over. You win.
2. What did you negotiate for when you accepted your current position?	If the answer is, "I didn't negotiate" or "I accepted the offer," proceed to question 3.
3. What do you think you should be paid for the job you do?	If the answer is, "I don't know, but what I am getting isn't nearly enough," proceed to question 4. If you have an amount in mind, return to question 2 and continue this frustrating loop until you learn to negotiate!
4. What are you doing that makes you worth more money?	If you have a concise list of skills, special knowledge areas, qualities, and experiences, proceed to question 5. If the answer is, "I'm not sure," return to question 1 and change your answer to yes. Then read on.
5. How will you negotiate for an increase?	If your answer is either of the following, read on: "I'm not sure how to ask for more." "I am uncomfortable asking for more."

I'm sure you get the point. Thanks for playing along.

We don't necessarily earn what we are worth; we earn what we believe we are worth and what we negotiate for.

This can be daunting for women because we really don't like to negotiate. When men hear a salary offer, they believe the negotiations have begun, and they actually look forward to it! The first offer is like the opening move in a chess game. Men hear it and say, "I need to earn at least…" When women receive a salary offer, they believe it is what it is. They politely say, "Thank you so much."

And it doesn't stop there. Men might ask for five separate things in a salary negotiation—anything from the starting salary to a flexible schedule and more vacation time. They may only get three of the five things they ask for, but they will leave the table feeling like they won.

The point is: men expect more from the negotiation. They believe more is available, and they believe they are worth more. The process is more natural for them—enjoyable even.

When I ask hiring managers about their experiences negotiating job offers, they confirm this. Women rarely negotiate. When they do, it's mainly about the money, and they seem uncomfortable—even apologetic—broaching the subject. Men definitely negotiate more often, ask for more inside of the negotiation, and appear perfectly comfortable if not downright pleased in the process.

It's not hard to understand why the majority of women struggle with negotiation. A quick review of challenges we discussed in the first chapter, the way women are socialized and the messages we grow up with, helps to explain why this is not always a natural skill. If negotiation is difficult for you, I hope you will remember it is a skill. With practice, skills can be learned and mastered. I hope you will be encouraged to step out of your comfort zone and try these strategies.

Let's begin with your own experience. What is the difference between the situations when you have asked for what you want or need, and when you haven't? The difference may come down to clarity, confidence, and control—knowing what you want, believing you deserve it, and feeling powerful enough to ask for it. In my experience the most successful negotiations happen when all three of these elements come together.

Why Don't We Ask for What We Want and Need?

Authors Linda Babcock and Sara Laschever discuss how women feel about negotiation and the price of their reluctance in the book *Women Don't Ask: Negotiation and the Gender Divide.*[1] From their research we learn:

✓ Women are four times less likely than men to initiate negotiations and more than twice as apprehensive about it.

✓ Men describe negotiating as a competition, like winning a ball game, while women think of it as a trip to the dentist.

✓ Women pay more for purchases to avoid negotiating.

✓ Men ask for more when negotiating and women ask for less. Even when they do negotiate, women believe less is available.

✓ Negotiating a starting salary makes a significant difference. Women who consistently negotiate earn at least $1 million more during their careers than women who don't.

✓ Women tend to undervalue their worth.

We won't always get what we ask for, and some of our negotiations will fail. That doesn't mean we should quit trying!

Sometimes we may feel like the woman in a recent workshop who said, "I don't speak up anymore. It doesn't do any good. I've learned to just do what they tell me."

Her whole demeanor was one of defeat and resignation—tired of the battle. A robot now, she simply follows orders. She has learned the wrong lesson from her negotiation experiences!

In the Bible, we are encouraged to ask and to keep asking: "Keep on asking, and you will receive what you ask for. Keep on seeking, and you will find. Keep on knocking, and the door will be opened to you" (Matthew 7:7, NLT).

The resiliency to keep asking may require us to change our approach—how we are asking. We may need to rethink what we're asking for, prepare more thoroughly, offer evidence, anticipate objections, consider other perspectives, and suggest alternatives.

When our negotiations fail, we may need to gracefully accept that and move on. Walking around with a giant chip on your shoulder is exhausting, unattractive, and very bad for posture. But a failed negotiation—or two or three or ten—doesn't mean we stop asking altogether.

In the example above, this woman stopped asking because it didn't seem to make a difference. In other cases, perhaps we don't even know what to ask for—we haven't clearly identified what we need. Sometimes we may not ask because deep down we believe we should be able to do it all without help. In that light, asking for help means we haven't done "our job." Perhaps the most tragic reason of all is we don't ask because we don't think we deserve.

Before we are free to ask, we may need to put a different frame around negotiation. Women often see negotiation as conflict or a fight. We don't like conflict, and we don't like to fight. That can make even the thought of negotiation agonizing.

What if you thought of negotiation as collaboration—the opportunity to explore alternatives and create more value for everyone involved? What if you saw negotiation as a creative, problem-solving process designed to explore less obvious solutions?

Perhaps one of the best ways to reframe negotiation is to think about what we give up when we don't negotiate and what we might gain if we do. A simple cost/benefit analysis may be in order.

Negotiation isn't just about money. That's just the beginning. There is more at stake here than the size of your paycheck. We can also negotiate for the things that make us worth more and things that make our jobs and lives more satisfying. Here's a short list of what we can—and should—negotiate for:

1. More challenging responsibility

2. More rewarding assignments

3. More authority

4. Greater flexibility or control in the way you do your job

5. Training and professional development

6. Resources and tools

7. Help at home

The benefits of negotiating are obvious. We get more of what we want and need more often. When we fail to negotiate, we set others and ourselves up for disappointment.

> Tammy works for a bank. She is an excellent salesperson, and her boss involves her in special business-development projects. As a result, she is often asked to work long and nontraditional hours. Tammy doesn't claim overtime or even keep track of these extra hours for two reasons: being asked feels like recognition, and she doesn't know how to bring it up. This pattern continues for about a year. Tammy is beginning to resent the amount of unpaid time she is working, and she resents her boss for taking such advantage of her.

When we fail to negotiate, it's possible, even likely, we will eventually feel taken advantage of. When that happens, we may "blame" others or the organization.

Ironically, some of the best negotiators I know are women. When I think about what sets them apart, they are very confident and knowledgeable. They ask without apology and with the expectation of getting what they ask for. Maybe the greatest difference is in how they feel about negotiating and what they believe it is. First, they believe everything is negotiable—they see options and alternatives others miss. Next, they see negotiation as a reasonable exchange of value. They don't think of negotiation as winning or losing.

Let's compare that with what is probably more typical.

Elizabeth is a Realtor in Seattle. She is hardworking, patient, and completely committed to her clients. We can learn a great deal from the negotiating lessons she learned—the hard way—early in her career.

"My clients were first-time home buyers," Elizabeth explains, "and I worked with them for six long months. They had a lot to learn, and so did I. After viewing dozens of homes, they found the perfect one. Then we promptly lost it in the negotiation.

"The home was older, and the inspection came in with a lengthy list of repairs. Some of these repairs were essential; others were recommendations and minor issues. After reviewing the inspection report with my clients, I asked them, 'What do you want the sellers to repair?' The clients said, 'Everything. We want them to fix everything.'

"Dutifully I went back to the sellers with the message. Visibly wincing I said, 'My buyers want you to repair everything noted in the inspection.' The sellers were stunned by what they felt was completely unreasonable. They simply replied, 'We have a backup offer on the house and we're going to take it.' Game over.

"At first I was so frustrated—and more than a little angry with my clients for being so unreasonable. Then it hit me. Not only had I failed to negotiate, I didn't even realize I was in a negotiation! I let myself become a messenger in the transaction—like a school girl passing notes in class!"

In this situation there were two negotiations happening simultaneously, and Elizabeth missed both of them. She failed to negotiate the inspection report with her own clients to reset their expectations and create a reasonable bottom line. And she failed to negotiate with the sellers to close the deal.

You may be thinking, "She's a Realtor, for heaven's sake. Her job is to negotiate!" That may be true, but can you relate to her experience?

- ✓ Have you ever missed an opportunity to negotiate?
- ✓ Have you ever paid too much or settled for not enough?
- ✓ Has your hard work ever been wasted because you weren't clear on your bottom line?
- ✓ Have you ever said yes when you should have said no?
- ✓ Have you ever agreed to something that you wished you hadn't?
- ✓ Have you walked away feeling as if you gave a whole lot more than you received?

We can't be too hard on Elizabeth. She teaches us that even in jobs where negotiation is an assumed skill, it's not an automatic one.

Elizabeth's negotiating lessons weren't finished. She still needed to learn the importance of creating a win-win. "I was so eager to please," she admits. "In one very memorable transaction, I proudly brought the sellers a full-price offer and a commitment from my client to close in record time.

"The sellers were thrilled. They thought I was a miracle worker. But when I went back to my client with the accepted offer, he said, 'Let me see if I understand: We are offering full price for this home *and* agreeing to close practically tomorrow. What exactly did I get in return for that?'"

Elizabeth did not have an answer. She had agreed to give extra value with a quick close, but she had not asked for anything in return. "The closing was very stressful because we had agreed on such a short time frame. My client was stomping mad every step of the way. He did not feel like he 'won' anything in the negotiation, and he reminded me of that daily."

The best negotiations are the ones in which everyone feels like a winner.

Where Logic and Emotion Meet

Inside every negotiation, two processes are at work: the psychological or emotional process, and the rational or logical process.[2]

EMOTIONAL (PSYCHOLOGICAL) PROCESS	LOGICAL (RATIONAL) PROCESS
• How comfortable we are in the negotiation • What we assume about this situation and our chances of success • How much we trust the others involved • What we perceive is at stake—what is to lose and what is to gain	• Analyzing the situation—critical thinking • Generating options and alternatives—creative thinking • Problem solving • Decision making

If there is a weakness on either side of this process, negotiations will suffer. I may be extremely comfortable in the negotiation, but if I fail to analyze the situation, I weaken my ability to negotiate substantially.

If we return to Elizabeth and the failed real-estate transaction, we can see breakdowns in both the emotional and the logical processes. Elizabeth wasn't confident in her negotiating role, and she didn't work with her clients to generate options and alternatives to creatively solve the problem. She came to the table with an ultimatum and discovered her clients had viable alternatives!

Know Your Bottom Line

Go into every negotiation knowing exactly what you want, knowing what you can't leave without, and knowing what your options are if the negotiations fail.

In the book *Getting to Yes: Negotiating Without Giving In,* authors Roger Fisher and William Ury give us the tool BATNA. Your BATNA is your "best alternative to a negotiated agreement."[3]

Think of your BATNA as a ruler, negotiation guide, or measuring stick. This ruler gives you the confidence to decide whether to accept or reject what is offered because you know what your alternatives are if you don't. When you are very clear about your alternatives, you protect yourself from agreeing to something that isn't in your best interest or rejecting terms that may be.

Using best alternatives as a guide, the general rule is to accept terms that are better than your BATNA and try to renegotiate terms that are not. Strengthen your negotiating position by strengthening your options. That just means more and better alternatives give you a stronger negotiating position.

Skilled negotiators also consider the options of others involved. What alternatives do they have if negotiations with you fail? The following case illustrates how important it is to understand the alternatives.

> Diane is a senior loan processor for a mortgage company. She has been with her firm for ten years. A competitor has offered her a 10 percent increase in salary. Today she met with her boss to ask for a 10 percent raise.
>
> Diane's best alternative is very strong. If she doesn't receive the raise she is asking for, she can resign and take the job offer. Using that as a guide, anything less than a 10 percent pay increase is unfavorable.

Diane's boss appears to have weaker alternatives. If she loses one of her most senior processors, she may have to replace the talent. That will impact productivity and service consistency; it will cost money. Unless she can improve her options, granting Diane's request may be the wise choice.

But what if options do exist? What if volume projections are down and Diane's boss can absorb the loss of a processor? Perhaps she can replace one senior processor with two junior processors and increase processing capacity. With these alternatives, perhaps she doesn't agree to the increase.

On the surface of this negotiation, the choices seem limited. Diane will either receive a raise or leave the company. Her boss will either grant the request or lose a valuable employee. These are win-lose or lose-win outcomes. How can these women create a win-win alternative?

Make the Pie Bigger

In negotiations there are two distinct strategies: distributive bargaining (claiming value) and integrative bargaining (creating value).[4]

Distributive bargaining is a win-lose strategy. Resources are generally fixed, and sides compete for pieces of the pie. With this strategy, each side of the negotiation is primarily concerned with maximizing its own interests—getting more of the pie—and claiming more value.

When distributive bargaining is used, negotiation tactics may include power plays like manipulation, force, and withholding information. Cards are held close to the chest, and the other side of the negotiation is considered the enemy. Here negotiation is a competition. There is one pie, and the goal is to get more pieces of it.

With integrative or collaborative bargaining, it is possible for both sides to win. In fact, that is the goal. We believe we can make the pie bigger. We can create more value. Sides are primarily concerned with maximizing joint interests, and tactics include information sharing, collaboration, brainstorming, and creative problem solving.

The real question becomes, "How can we both get more of what we want and need in this situation?" Rather than an adversary, the other side becomes a problem-solving partner.

DISTRIBUTIVE (COMPETITIVE) BARGAINING STRATEGIES	INTEGRATIVE (COLLABORATIVE) BARGAINING STRATEGIES
The first offer is an "anchor" and sets the bargaining range. Come in high!	Share information about your circumstances.
Do not disclose significant information about your circumstances.	Work to understand what is important to others involved. What are their primary concerns, hopes, fears, or objectives?
Don't let the other side see a weakness.	Explain what is important to you, and why.
Make it clear you have other options.	Discuss preferences and options openly.
Let them know you can, and may, walk at any time.	Talk about ways you can add more value to the deal.

Integrative bargaining uses disclosure to connect with the needs and goals of everyone involved. It openly invites collaboration. Picture yourself moving to the same side of the table—partnering to find a solution that meets the primary interests of both sides. You may even declare it! You might say, "I want to understand your goals here. I want us to find a solution that works for both of us."

Sometimes we can create more value in our negotiations by offering something we value less in exchange for something we value more. Think about the case of the employee we risk losing. What are some things Diane's boss could throw in? What might her senior processor greatly value that she can afford to give away?

Diane's manager may be unable to offer a 10 percent increase. Perhaps she can only offer 5 percent. Or she might make the pie bigger by offering:

✓ An additional week of paid vacation

✓ Specialized training

✓ A more flexible schedule

✓ The visibility and recognition of working on a strategic team to improve processes

Diane's boss needs to make this negotiation more than a discussion about money. If she views this as a problem to solve *with* her employee, she can turn it into collaboration.

When You Give Value, Say So

By the way, when you give something in a negotiation, make sure the other side knows they are receiving real value.

> I learned this from watching Liz, a successful entrepreneur who has built a thriving training company. When she throws something into the deal to add value, she candidly tells the client, "I am giving you something here. It has real value, and I'm giving it to you."

If you give something away without declaring the value, you may create an unrealistic expectation for future negotiations. Instead of creating value you can draw on, you have created the expectation for accommodation.

The Enemies of Collaboration

Women can be great negotiators because we are relationship oriented and collaborative. These are often natural skills. We are good at connecting with what is important to others, but collaboration does have enemies. It is impossible to invite a spirit of collaboration when we:

- ✓ Defend positions rather than work to understand interests
- ✓ Fail to locate what matters most to everyone involved
- ✓ Are overly concerned with the needs of others at the expense of our own needs—that's not negotiation, that's accommodation
- ✓ Assume someone must win and someone must lose
- ✓ Allow emotions to dominate the process
- ✓ Let it get personal

To demonstrate the dynamics of collaboration, I often ask audience members to "choose a partner; move anything that will spill, break, or hurt you; and prepare to arm wrestle!" With a groan, they move into position. Next I tell them they have twelve seconds to win. In fact, I want them to win as often as they can in the time allowed. To spur them on, I ask them to pretend they will receive $1,000 each time they win.

The transformation is amazing! The gentlest of people become the fiercest of contenders. Even in this pretend negotiation, everyone wants to win! The twelve seconds are a complete frenzy. Some people are winning, some are losing, and some pairs are strained in a red-faced draw. When I call time, some don't want to quit because there has been no winner.

When I ask for the winners to stand, they do so proudly. Some of them have pummeled their partners repeatedly, and they are quite pleased with themselves—until they hear the true solution.

What if you didn't see this as a win or lose situation? What if you had collaborated with your partner? What if you had asked, "How can we both win more?"

The solution is simple. Let's not resist each other. I will let you win and you will let me win. We will do that as fast as we can—arms flying back and forth for twelve seconds. Another groan fills the room as people realize they completely missed the opportunity to win more by competing less.

Focus on Why Rather Than What

In negotiation, your position is what you want. Your interests are why you want that—why it matters to you. It is the underlying need. If you focus primarily on positions in a negotiation—what you want or what others want—you limit the possibilities tremendously. You box yourself in and set yourself up for a win-lose or lose-win situation.

Seasoned negotiators look for integrative solutions, and those can be found by understanding the interests of everyone involved.

As you build your negotiation skills, you will learn people are people after all, and they are essentially concerned with, interested in, and looking for the same things you are. Remember Abraham Maslow's hierarchy of needs? He contended that once our basic needs are met, we look for ways to be more secure, then to belong, then to achieve, and finally to reach our fullest potential.[5]

This can be a useful model when you think about what motivates people in a negotiation. If I am worried about enough money to pay my bills, that need will drive me. Once that need is met, other things may become more important to me—the need for recognition, challenge, and achievement.

In our sample case, Diane's position is a 10 percent raise. That is what she wants. But do we really know why?

Maybe Diane wants to earn more or maybe she *needs* to earn

more. Something may have changed in her life, causing a financial strain. Perhaps the money is not the issue at all—the real need is to feel more valued and recognized. Maybe after ten years with the company she believes she has capped out financially. There is no room for her to grow—to reach her full potential.

Diane's position is clear: she wants a raise. Before meeting with Diane, her boss would be wise to consider the underlying interests, develop a plan to discover what is most important to her, and look for integrative solutions—a win for the organization and a win for Diane.

Ask Questions to Discover What Matters Most

As you prepare to negotiate, you can make some assumptions about what is important to the others involved. As you begin to negotiate, you will want to verify, clarify, and invite people to talk about what matters most. Equip yourself with questions:

✓ What is your primary concern?

✓ What is most important to you?

✓ Why is this so important to you?

Ultimately, negotiation is about creating and exchanging value. These are also the instruments of influence. In the book *Influence Without Authority*, Allan Cohen and David Bradford frame influence as exchange. There is something you need or want, and you must find something of value to trade for it.[6] The law of reciprocity—the Golden Rule—is at work here.

When we give something of value, people are more inclined to give something of value in return. Before you ask for something in a negotiation, consider what you have to give.

> Kathy, an incredible Realtor in South Texas, intuitively understands the law of reciprocity. She was negotiating a large transaction with an attorney. When he asked her

which title company she would be using, she immediately recognized an opportunity to give. She said, "If you have someone you would like to give this business to, let's go with that firm. This may be a good way for you to build or strengthen that relationship."

The attorney was grateful. He did have someone in mind—someone who had just referred business to him. This was his opportunity to return the favor. Then Kathy asked for something in return—a big something actually.

Without batting an eye, she asked, "Who will be paying for the title policy?" I'll let you guess who picked up that bill.

What you have to give is your currency. And most of us have more currency and more kinds of currency than we may realize.

Find your currencies by thinking about what you have to offer. Do you have specialized knowledge, information, or skills? Can you give appreciation, support, recognition, or visibility? Do you have contacts or other resources you can share? From time to time it's worthwhile to take inventory.

1. What currencies do you have?

2. How much currency do you have?

3. Which currencies do you need to develop?

Grow your influence and your ability to negotiate with confidence by growing the kinds and amounts of currency you have to offer. In the next chapter, influence will also be a key concept as you learn to lead from your current position.

High-Impact Ideas

✓ We don't necessarily earn what we are worth. We earn what we believe we are worth and what we negotiate for.

✓ The ability and willingness to negotiate may come down to three factors: clarity, confidence, and control—knowing what you want, believing you deserve it, and feeling powerful enough to ask for it.

✓ We may need to mentally reframe negotiation. Women often see negotiation as conflict or a fight. We don't like conflict, and we don't like to fight. That makes the negotiation process agonizing. What if we saw negotiation as collaboration—the opportunity to explore alternatives and create more value for everyone involved?

✓ Inside every negotiation, two processes are at work—the psychological or emotional process, and the rational or logical process. If there is a weakness on either side of this process, negotiations will suffer.

✓ The best negotiations are the ones in which everyone feels like a winner.

✓ When we fail to negotiate, it's possible—even likely—we will eventually feel taken advantage of. When that happens we may blame the organization.

✓ Go into every negotiation knowing exactly what you want, knowing what you can't leave without, and knowing what your options are if negotiations fail.

✓ Look for ways to make the "pie bigger" to create more value.

✓ When you give something in a negotiation, make sure the other side knows they are receiving real value.

✓ Focus on interests, not positions. Find out what people want in the negotiation, but don't stop there. Find out why they want it.

✓ Integrative solutions are often found in underlying interests or needs.

✓ Before asking for something in a negotiation, consider what you have to give. When you do ask for something in return, ask *without* apology and *with* the expectation of getting what you've ask for.

✓ Increase your influence by managing the kinds of and the amount of currency you have to exchange.

Questions for Reflection

What should you be negotiating for in your current position?

_____

_____

_____

What negotiation opportunities are you missing?

_____

_____

_____

How can you make your pie bigger?

_____

_____

_____

Action Items

Interview a great negotiator. Ask this person to share their best lessons learned with you. Ask them for examples of how they have created more value and how they have invited collaboration.

In your next negotiating opportunity, openly declare your goal to create a win-win outcome. Reach—I mean *really* reach—to understand what the other party wants and needs *before* talking about what you want and need.

Take an inventory of your currencies. Choose one currency you want to have or have more of. Develop an action plan to increase your influence ability.

Chapter 6

COMMANDMENT 5:
Lead From Your Current Position

Years ago I had a performance problem with one of the most likeable people I've ever met. Frank was just out of college—full of potential and charisma, with nothing whatsoever to back it up. His greatest skill turned out to be window dressing—creating a fabulous impression without delivering anything of real value.

It was easy to understand how Frank had managed his way through life so far. He was very charming, and I could see him successfully manipulating people and circumstances to create an appearance of success. Perhaps for the first time in his life he was actually being held accountable for results, and it wasn't going well.

Frank was completely unaffected when I invited him to my office to discuss his performance. Now it was my turn to be frank, and I was as I explained my frustration with his lack of focus, disappointment in his work ethic, and concern with his personal motivation. He shrugged nonchalantly and said, "I didn't go to school for this. I went to school for your job."

That day Frank was freed up for a new opportunity.

I **DIDN'T FIRE** Frank for wanting my job. I fired him because he wasn't willing to earn it. He made a fatal mistake believing that leadership is something you "get." It isn't. Leadership is something you are.

Leadership isn't a title, and titles don't guarantee leadership. I have known many people with impressive titles who didn't understand the first thing about leadership, and I've had the pleasure of meeting extraordinary leaders without any title at all. Some of the most powerful people I meet aren't the decision makers—they are the people who influence the decision makers!

Ask any leader and they will tell you, titles and position don't magically fix every problem and automatically pave the way to success. In his book *The 360-Degree Leader,* John Maxwell exposes the "freedom myth." This is when we mistakenly believe that once we get to the top we are free of all limits, our problems are solved, and we have arrived.[1] Perhaps you have a title, maybe even a big one. I'll bet if we could talk to you, you would say the title is what goes on the organization chart. Leadership is something else altogether.

The First Person You Must Learn to Lead Is You

Personal leadership and mastery speak to work ethic, integrity, consistency, initiative, and discipline. It's doing the right thing even when no one is looking. Strike that. It is doing the right thing, the effective thing, *especially* when no one is looking!

When I ask people if they would like to make more money, I always hear a resounding *yes*! But how often do we, consciously or unconsciously, reverse the process? I've actually heard people say, "When I make more, I'll do more." My response to these precious people is, "You'll never make more until you are *worth* more!"

You have to *be* something before you can *get* something. Maybe we don't actually say it, but are there times when we hold back the best of who we are because "that's not our job"? Admit it. Haven't you ever thought, "That's not my problem," or "I don't get paid enough to put up with this!"? OK, I'll go first. I have.

When it comes to personal leadership, we can't wait for the position to demonstrate it. We can't wait for the promotion to make the difference, because the difference is what makes the promotion.

> I once had the pleasure of hearing a compelling message from an executive at the new AT&T, addressing a group of high-potential employees. I will always remember something she said: "The first thing is to nail the job you have. Then look for ways to extend your reach—to have a broader impact on the organization."
>
> This resonated with me. Nail your job. The one you have. The one you dressed up, interviewed, and prayed for. Then look for ways to do more, be more, and make a greater difference.

Here are some ways to nail your job and lead from where you are.

Become a Time-Management Expert

Personal leadership begins with who you are and becomes what you do. Ultimately what you do *becomes* who you are. This is a perpetual cycle of *becoming,* and if you don't manage it, it will manage you.

The most successful people are also the most productive ones. They are extremely focused on the actions that produce results, and they are decisive about where to invest their time. If you sincerely want to achieve more, become more valuable to the organization, and enjoy your work more, you simply must become an expert time manager.

Until you do, you will struggle around at a level of performance that does not reflect your true potential. You will be derailed by what is trivial and miss what is essential, you'll run in constant crisis mode—which is a perfect formula for burnout—and your schedule will be driven by things you will never control.

You can't manage time. That's just crazy. Time marches on with or without your permission. Your only hope is to manage yourself in time.

Make Room for Time

Imagine time is a house with four rooms, and all of your activities, tasks, and commitments must be placed into one of them. Each room has a name, and the name is really a goal.

The first room is called Maximize. Here you will place all of the things that make you better—the actions you can take to be more prepared, informed, knowledgeable, effective, and valuable. *The goal is to spend more time in this room.*

Into the second room you will gather the things that cause you to react. These are situations and circumstances that throw you into the frenzy of crisis mode. Call this room Minimize, because you want to reduce the amount of time you spend here. Stress also lives in this room. Incidentally, when you spend more time in the first room, you end up here less often.

Next is the room for everything that steals your time. You'll recognize the activities that belong in here because they don't add anything. They just take. This is where gossip, perfectionism, negativity, blame storming, fear, and worry live. This room is called Eliminate. If you pay close attention, you'll be surprised how often you go into this room and how much time you actually spend here. I've met people who stay here almost all of the time. I'll bet a few names and faces come to your mind as well.

The last room is called Manage. It's a place for meetings, interruptions, and communications. This is where conference calls, voice mail, e-mail, and "do you have a minute?" live. Some of these are essential and some, quite frankly, are not. You must learn to tell the difference so you can put them in the rooms where they really belong. Quite often this is the most cramped room in the house, and you may find yourself climbing over things to search for what is lost in the chaos.

With your first assessment, you are likely to find some activities living in the wrong room, and you may discover the room called Maximize is nearly empty. The goal is to take inventory, put things in the proper place, and spend your time where you will realize the greatest return.

A Dozen Good Strategies to Maximize Your Time

1. Make appointments with yourself—and actually keep them. Block out time to work on your projects, and treat this time just as you would an appointment with your boss.

2. Plan 60 percent of your time and leave 40 percent open to flex with shifting priorities, interruptions, and the unexpected. You will never completely eliminate interruptions, and priorities will move on you without warning. The key is to build flexibility into your day so you can shift gears without abandoning your plan.

3. Know your top three priorities every day. Everything won't get done. Make sure your top three priorities do.

4. Keep your daily task list to ten items. More than ten probably isn't realistic, and that's demotivating.

5. Set aside time to plan on a yearly, monthly, weekly, and daily basis.

6. Start your day in the room called Maximize. This is where you set goals, plan, and prepare. If you don't start here, you may never get here.

7. Turn interruptions into appointments. Just because something is screaming, ringing, or otherwise demanding your

attention does not make it a top priority. Plug interruptions into the 40 percent flex time you've built into your day.

8. Beat procrastination by working ahead of the deadline. Every day discipline yourself to work for thirty minutes on something that isn't due. By the time it's due, it'll be done—or very close.

9. Use a time management system. Pick what works for you. It may be a traditional organizer or something higher tech. Whatever you choose, keep it up to date and keep it with you at all times.

10. Once you have a plan, protect it! Learn how to say no.

11. Be especially careful when asked to make future commitments. Because they are far off in time, people tend to make those agreements without fully considering the impact. Before you know it, the promise you made weeks ago has arrived, and your plate is spilling over...again.

12. Diagnose your day. Keep a time log for several days to see where your time is really going. This is not the most exciting assignment, but it's one of the most profitable recommendations I can make.

SAMPLE TIME LOG			
TASK	PRIORITY	DURATION	OBSERVATIONS
What did you do?	Which priority did this task impact?	How long did you spend on this task?	What did you notice? What did you achieve? What did you learn? What would you change? Which room are you in?

My time management mentors have been people like Dr. Stephen Covey, Brian Tracy, and David Allen. They can be your time experts as well. If you plan to become a student of time, allow me to introduce the faculty and the textbooks.

1. Brian Tracy, *The Psychology of Achievement* (Niles, IL: Nightingale-Conant, 1998).

2. Stephen R. Covey, *First Things First* (New York: Fireside, 1994).

3. David Allen, *Getting Things Done: The Art of Stress-Free Productivity* (New York: Penguin, 2001).

Develop a Broader Understanding of the Organization

I think it's possible—common even—to work in a vacuum, check off tasks, complete assignments, and meet deadlines without really understanding how the machine runs, what is produced, and how the end product works.

Knowing how you fit—how your work fits—into the bigger picture is really important. When you understand the flow of the work and the broader objectives of the organization, you work in context. That means you can:

✓ Find ways to streamline and simplify

✓ Make better decisions about where to invest your time

✓ Know when and how to reach across the aisle and partner with others more effectively

✓ Understand the implications of your decisions—how they affect people down the line or across the hall

✓ Appreciate people and processes. You'll understand what your requests mean for others. What seems to you like a simple request may be more complicated than you realize. Or you may find a small change in your process makes a huge difference from someone down the line.

Get to know the organization, your products and services better. Work in context.

Know Your Impact

Check for alignment between what you are doing and what matters most to the organization. The more aligned you are with the goals and priorities of the organization, the more valuable and relevant you become.

The City of Irving, Texas, has made this a corporate discipline. They publish a brochure listing the city's strategic plan for the next three to five years.[2] It consists of ten goals and seventy-seven strategies that address future city initiatives. Employees receive a copy so they can make the connection between their assignments and the initiatives they personally impact. If they can't make that connection, they are encouraged to ask the question, "How does my job impact the priorities of the city? Where does this assignment fit on the list?" What a marvelous example of corporate accountability!

I hope you are fortunate enough to work for an organization that deliberately connects the dots between what you do and the difference you make. My experience tells me that most people don't. We will probably need to make the connection for ourselves. In that case, here's what you can do to understand your impact:

- ✓ Find out what the key success indicators are and ask yourself how you impact those results on a daily basis.

- ✓ Ask your boss, "In the next thirty to ninety days, what are your top three priorities, and how can I personally impact them?" This is a show-stopping, value-raising, set-yourself-immediately-apart question! You'll want to ask this question frequently because, as you well know, priorities can quickly shift.

✓ Study the strategic plan for your organization and look for ways to get plugged in.

✓ If your assignments don't seem relevant to the long term, initiate the conversation and recommend ways you can become more connected to results.

When you understand your impact, you've made a leap that many employees never will. You've already begun to raise the standard.

Raising the Standard

Every day we have the choice to do just what is required of us or something more. We can mark the time and treat our jobs like a prison sentence, or we can bring more creativity, more energy, and more passion to it.

Raising the standard, then, is a personal choice. It is doing your best work every day—even when you don't feel like it. You raise the standard when you:

✓ Separate yourself from people who are satisfied with what is mediocre and average and surround yourself with people who want to, and believe they can, accomplish something extraordinary

✓ Cultivate an optimistic, solutions-oriented attitude

✓ Exceed performance expectations

✓ Look, sound, and behave professionally

✓ Fiercely guard your integrity

✓ Demonstrate loyalty

✓ Deliver the highest quality work

✓ Take responsibility for your successes and failures

✓ Set an exceptional example

✓ Invest yourself in team accomplishments—become a shareholder in success

When I ask successful women for specific examples of how they raise the standard at work, they say:

✓ "I go out of my way to help others in my group. I am proactive in asking how I can help."

✓ "I don't attend after-hours events too often. When I do, I remember that I am representing my company."

✓ "I let people know I'll do whatever it takes to get the job done. I'll come in early, work through lunch, or work late. People know they can count on me for results."

✓ "I am not afraid to fall because I realize I have the strength to pick myself up and carry on with integrity and honesty."

✓ "I keep my boss informed of work issues and welcome input and advice."

✓ "I put myself out there as a problem solver. People know they can come to me for solutions."

✓ "No matter how frustrated I may be with the company or my boss, I never complain about it at work."

I encourage you to think about how you can raise the standard. What can you do to put a topspin on the ball and set yourself apart? Whatever those action items turn out to be, consistency is essential and initiative is a requirement.

Seven Ways to Demonstrate Extreme Initiative

1. *Make it unnecessary for your boss to ask.* Initiate follow-up and demonstrate follow-through with your assignments and projects. Make sure your boss doesn't have to chase you down and search you out to get an update and check on a deadline.

2. *Communicate goals and priorities.* Give your boss a copy of your action plan at the beginning of each week. Highlight your top priorities and deliverables. At the end of the week, debrief your results. You can do this in person or in writing. Keep it simple and make it a consistent practice.

3. *Adopt a "no surprises" policy.* Bosses really do hate surprises when it comes to issues and results. Make it a personal policy that your boss will never be surprised by bad news.

   When my son was in school, we had a "no surprises" policy in our home. We told him: "If you get into trouble, we better hear it from you first." More than once he negotiated with the principal for a sixty-second head start to the telephone!

   The point is, when the news is bad, make sure your boss hears it from you first.

4. *Present solutions.* When you bring your boss issues, bring options and recommendations to go with them.

   You can take this to another level by seeking out solutions. Make continuous improvement a personal priority. Look for what costs too much, takes too long, or what is poor in quality. Do some research and develop recommendations for improvement.

5. *Ask for more.* Ask for a more challenging assignment. Volunteer to work on a special project.

6. *Adapt to your boss's communication style.* Does your boss prefer the highlights or the details? Does she like to be updated by e-mail, voice mail, or in person? Does your boss enjoy casual conversation, or does she hope and pray you will get to the point soon? Adjust your communication style to match these preferences and watch your credibility grow.

7. *Find a need and adopt a cause.* Look for a corporate cause and get behind it. Be the voice for something that will make the organization and the people in it better.

The Hardest Person to Manage May Be the One You Work For

Sometimes the most difficult person we manage is our boss. (I can almost hear the giant *Amen!* as you read that.) It is true. Bosses can be hard to manage, but manage them we must. When we don't, we can expect:

✓ Unrealistic deadlines

✓ Unclear expectations

✓ Ambiguous assignments

✓ Faltering support

✓ Generalized reactivity

✓ Defensive interactions

✓ To feel isolated, as in, it's you against the whole world

No one can expect to work effectively and enjoy their work with all of that going on.

You take the first step toward managing your boss the moment you realize you need to. From there, focus on building credibility and confidence by absolutely nailing your job. Beyond that you'll find plenty of opportunities to demonstrate awareness and practice your negotiation, communication, and empowerment skills.

Below are some if-and-then scenarios that may help you diagnose and treat difficult boss situations.

IF YOUR BOSS IS…	THEN…
UNORGANIZED	• Build in reminders. • Confirm priorities frequently. • Make your plan more visible. • Offer to take something off her too-full plate.
REACTIVE	• Help your boss anticipate issues and develop contingency plans. • Ask questions to help your boss think proactively; for example, "What if…?" "How should we plan to…?" "How can I help you prepare for…?"
UNAVAILABLE OR MISSING	• Find ways to work more independently. • Find alternative ways to communicate. • Keep communication flowing from your end with written updates and status reports. • Be prepared to discuss key issues—who knows when a missing boss may reappear. • Be concise, because you may only have thirty seconds to explain your situation or circumstance.
MAKING A BAD DECISION	• Provide recommendations with supporting data. • Use facts, not feelings, to voice your concerns. • Present a compelling case for the right decision. • Once you've made your stand, respect your boss's decision—even if you disagree with it—and move on. • Down the line, if presented with the opportunity, you may think, "I told you so," but you should resist saying it.
INCOMPETENT	• Demonstrate loyalty. Do what you can to make your boss look good, and never complain to co-workers. • Ask your boss for what you need to be successful. • Become more of a resource. • Seek advice from a mentor.

IF YOUR BOSS IS...	THEN...
A CONTROL FREAK	• Make your plan more visible. • Share information. • Focus on building trust and credibility. • Position yourself as a partner. • Negotiate for more latitude.
A COMPLETE JERK	• Turn off the "jerk filter" in your brain and think of your boss as a customer. • You aren't required to like your boss, but you aren't allowed to undermine, sabotage, or organize a campaign to overthrow her. • Ask accountable questions: "How am I contributing to the problem?" "What does my boss need?" "How can I invite a different response from my boss?" • Understand that you are in one of those accept, change, or leave situations. You have choices.

If you are in a "bad boss" situation, take the time to diagnose the issues, look for root causes, and develop a plan to be more effective. Focus on your responses, not your boss's behavior. You absolutely do not want to get lost in the dysfunction! If you are currently wandering around in that maze, raise a flag! Run the scenario by a mentor. If you don't have a mentor, hold on. I'll show you how to get one in the next chapter.

Working for a bad boss can erode confidence. Over time you may begin to feel powerless and trapped—questioning yourself and forgetting who you are. If that is where you are right now, this may be a good time to review Commandment 2. You are not powerless, and you do have options.

By the way, if reading this made you appreciate your great boss even more, go thank them! Someday you may even want to thank a bad boss. If we allow it, we can learn the most extraordinary things from the most difficult situations. I learned from my experience with a very bad boss that a bad leader isn't a good excuse for ineffectiveness. In other words, I can't wait for a manager to be a good leader to be effective myself.

All too often I see people waiting to take the lead, hesitating behind the line. I cannot tell you how often I've heard this kind of whining at conferences around the world:

- ✓ "I wish my boss was here. He really needs this."

- ✓ "This is all great stuff, but it won't work until it comes from the top of the organization."

- ✓ "We can try some of these strategies, but until we get more management support, it won't have much effect."

This makes me crazy!

Determine to make the difference you can, where you are, starting now. Don't wait for perfect conditions, effective managers, or even complete support. Be the difference, or at least the beginning of the difference.

I like grassroots initiatives. It is exciting to see people at all levels of an organization see a need or an opportunity, take ownership, and do something about it. I look for personal leadership everywhere I go. And I find the most extraordinary examples. These are people who didn't wait for someone else to make something good happen:

- ✓ Elizabeth, who works for a large, mostly male organization, asked a compelling question, "What can we do to support and develop women in this organization?" That question, asked of the right person in the right moment, inspired the Women's Initiative Network (WIN) for her organization.

- ✓ Natalie is deeply concerned about the young women in her community who settle for less and fail to reach for more. She has spent the last year developing a vision, a plan, and a network to support it. Momentum is building around her vision to assist women making the transition from high school to higher education. As a result of her efforts, women will dream bigger, achieve more, and stop settling for less than they were designed for.

✓ Kari suggested and implemented language studies in the cafeteria at her work. Now if you want to learn or practice Spanish, Italian, French, or Chinese, pack your lunch, choose a table, and immerse yourself in that language for an hour each day.

✓ Margie wanted to improve her presentation skills. She initiated a presentation club at work. The club has received a great deal of corporate recognition and has become a valuable resource for anyone wanting to develop confidence and communication skills.

Each of these women recognized a need and turned it into an opportunity. What is even more compelling is how they involved others to build momentum around their ideas. They created synergy and made others shareholders in the idea. This is what leaders do!

What Leadership Looks Like on You

There are dozens of things leaders do—some are intuitive; some are pure discipline. If I were asked to create a short list of the most significant leadership attributes and abilities, I'd say the most effective leaders:

✓ Create extreme focus around what really matters

✓ Make progress visible to create momentum and traction on the way to a goal

✓ Make the work meaningful, so people have a real sense of purpose in the work they do

✓ Equip and enable people for success

✓ Share information

✓ Build trust at every level

✓ Develop resiliency in themselves and others—the ability to bounce back even in the face of adversity

✓ Raise performance expectations

✓ Design opportunities for personal and professional growth

✓ Connect people to a compelling vision

✓ Recognize and reward excellence

These are some of the things we expect from leaders—what we want and need from them. What if you were to reverse the list and ask yourself a new set of questions? From the perspective of personal leadership, these aren't things we expect from others. Instead, they become tactics to lead from your current position.

If you asked me, "How can I lead from here?" I would answer your question with these. How can you...

✓ Become more focused on what really matters?

✓ Make your progress or the progress of your team more visible?

✓ Find more purpose and meaning in your work?

✓ Equip and enable yourself for success?

✓ Get the information you need to be effective?

✓ Build more trust and credibility?

✓ Demonstrate greater resiliency?

✓ Set a higher standard of performance?

✓ Develop and practice new skills?

✓ Have a greater impact on the long-term vision of the organization?

✓ Market your results more effectively?

Your answers to these questions mark the path to personal leadership. This is your action plan. When you find ways to lead from your current position, you have started constructing a bridge to your future.

High-Impact Ideas

✓ When it comes to personal leadership, we can't wait for the position to demonstrate it. We can't wait for the promotion to make the difference, because the difference is what makes the promotion.

✓ Nail your job. Then look for ways to extend your reach.

✓ Become a time-management expert.

✓ Knowing how you fit, how your work fits into the bigger picture, is really important. When you understand the flow of the work and the broader objectives of the organization, you work in context.

✓ Check for alignment between what you are doing and what matters most to the organization. The more aligned you are with the goals and priorities of the organization, the more valuable and relevant you become.

✓ Demonstrate extreme initiative.

✓ The hardest person to manage may be the one you work for. Manage your boss by understanding their working style, communication preferences, and even their weaknesses.

✓ A bad boss isn't a good excuse for being ineffective.

✓ If you are in a bad-boss situation, take the time to diagnose the issues, look for root causes, and develop a plan to be more effective.

✓ Involve others to build momentum around your ideas. Create synergy and turn people into shareholders.

✓ Turn the attributes of leadership into questions you ask of yourself. The answers become tactics to lead from your current position.

Questions for Reflection

How aligned are you with the priorities of the organization?

_____

_____

_____

How can you raise your personal standard?

_____

_____

_____

What can you do to manage your boss more effectively?

_____

_____

_____

Action Items

Identify one way you can demonstrate extreme initiative at work.

Review the list of tactics to maximize your time. Choose three to focus on.

Make a list of the things you expect from a leader. Turn that list into a set of questions and ask them of yourself. How can you demonstrate these attributes from your current position?

Chapter 7

COMMANDMENT 6:
Build a Bridge to the Future

Karen's company just hired a new manager from outside the organization. She wasn't even considered for the position. As she updates her résumé and scans the classifieds, she wonders, "Why didn't they ask me to apply?"

Catherine isn't interested in climbing a corporate ladder. She doesn't want a promotion, but she would like more challenge.

Julie has a great job, and she does it well. The problem is, she has no idea where she's going. There isn't a clear path, and she has no career plan.

FOR SOME THE future is a promotion—advancing to the next step. For others, advancement isn't the goal. In any case, growth is an imperative. You must be growing in the job you have. Staying where you are, as you are, is a prescription for becoming obsolete. All of us must build a bridge to the future.

The paradox is that women become so skilled at taking care of others, we may fail to take care of ourselves with clear goals and a well-defined plan. In this chapter, you are invited to create a vision of where you want to be in the future. With that destination in focus, you are ready to create a road map of the competencies, experiences, and credentials required to get there.

The time to prepare for your next opportunity is right now. Once your company has posted an open position, it's probably too late. Hiring managers will jump through the required hoops to fill a position, but chances are they've already made a choice. (That may sound unfair, but it's honest.) To get ahead of that curve, look for and ask for the experiences and exposures that will make you the top-of-mind, natural choice *before* a position opens.

You may ask for the opportunity to develop a budget or manage a project, solve a business problem, analyze a work flow, or make a formal presentation. Perhaps you can participate in strategic planning, work on a special task force, or lead a team meeting. Look for ways to demonstrate leadership capabilities—the ability to think strategically, communicate effectively, forge a team, and develop others.

Two important things happen when you search out experiences like these: you prepare for the future, and you send a message. The message reads, "Think of me when there is an opportunity."

Bring the Future Into Focus

Developing a career plan begins with a great deal of personal reflection and a gap analysis—comparing where you are now with where you want to be in the future. Typically career plans look ahead at least five years. Some reach even further into the future.

As you begin this process, be bold! Practice unlimited thinking. Don't worry in the beginning about *how* you will get there. Once you have defined your career objectives you will isolate the gaps, develop action steps, anticipate obstacles, and identify the resources you need.

The following questions will walk you through the process of building a career plan.

1. *Where do you want to be in five years?* Be as detailed as possible. What is the position? What are you earning? What do you love about the work you are doing? What impact are you having?

2. *Where are you now?* Describe your current position, job responsibilities, and compensation. What do you love about your job? What don't you love about it?

3. *What are your skills and strengths today?* This is not the time to be humble. List the skills you will need in your future position. What will be expected of you?

4. *What is your current educational and experiential profile?* When it comes to experience, think beyond any positions you've held. This question is asking you to reflect on your experience in those positions. Think about your assignments, projects, and achievements. What did you do? What did you learn? How did you make a difference?

5. *How do others perceive you now—both positively and negatively?* Make a list of how those perceptions will impact your plan. What are you known for today? What do you want to be known for?

6. *What are the gaps between where you are and where you want to be?* Once you've created this sketch, compare your current reality with the future you have imagined.

7. *What can you do to move closer to your career vision?* Your action plan builds a bridge from the present to

the future. It specifically addresses the gaps. Focus on actions you personally control. Break large action items into smaller, more manageable chunks. This will give you a greater sense of accomplishment and allow you to get traction and build momentum.

8. *What will be the hardest part of your development plan?* Anticipate the obstacles you will encounter and how you will overcome them. Be aware of what could keep you from achieving your goal. Know how to remove these barriers or minimize their impact on your plan.

9. *Whom do you know or need to meet who will support your plan and make it more possible?* List the resources you will need to be successful. These might include time, money, information, and people. Remember to make a budget for your career plan.

Using a table like the one below may help you construct a more comprehensive plan.

	WHAT IS THE CURRENT REALITY?	WHAT DO YOU WANT THE FUTURE TO LOOK LIKE?	WHAT IS THE DISTANCE BETWEEN WHERE AND THERE?	BUILD A BRIDGE WITH ACTION STEPS.	BRAINSTORM POTENTIAL BARRIERS AND RESOURCES.
Position Responsibilities and Compensation					
Skills and Strengths					

	WHAT IS THE CURRENT REALITY?	WHAT DO YOU WANT THE FUTURE TO LOOK LIKE?	WHAT IS THE DISTANCE BETWEEN WHERE AND THERE?	BUILD A BRIDGE WITH ACTION STEPS.	BRAINSTORM POTENTIAL BARRIERS AND RESOURCES.
Education and Experience					
Perspectives and Perceptions					

Your approach may be a little different if you want to grow in the job you have. Here are some questions you can use to take care of yourself with a professional development plan.

✓ What skills are you adding to yourself?

✓ What have you learned in the last six months, and how are you applying that to your work?

✓ How are you personally investing in your professional development?

✓ What skills will you need in one, three, and five years?

✓ How are you making yourself more valuable to your employer?

✓ How are you preparing yourself for future challenges and opportunities of your position?

A Study in Becoming High Potential

A great deal of the work I do is in the area of talent management—the development of high-potential people and programs. In talent management terms, high potential means I am taking very good care of what has been entrusted to me, I demonstrate extreme initiative, and I have the potential to grow and add even more value to the organization.

One of the most rewarding exercises in personal account-ability and professional development I've ever seen happened with a group in Dallas, Texas.

This group was comprised of men and women who were given the opportunity to participate in a series of learning experiences. These experiences included professional development workshops, mentoring, and special projects. The program was 100 percent self-selected. These people weren't picked randomly by management—tapped on the shoulder and called high potential. Everyone in the organization was invited to participate. The people involved are the ones who stepped up—literally.

One of the projects they accepted was very risky. They interviewed a panel of executives to identify the attributes of success. Using the attributes discovered, they developed a feedback tool—a survey designed to compare themselves against that benchmark.

The survey was electronically delivered to their supervisors, managers, and group executives. The results were then used to create personal action plans.

Talk about taking personal risk! Here are some of the accountable questions they posed:

- ✓ How promotable am I?
- ✓ How much do you trust me?
- ✓ Do I demonstrate extreme initiative?

✓ Do I accept and learn from my failures?

✓ How flexible am I?

✓ Do I seek opportunities to advance my career?

✓ Am I a valuable resource, someone you want on your team?

✓ How can I become more valuable to this organization?

✓ How can I become more promotable?

✓ Have I communicated my career goals?

It took a great deal of courage to ask for and graciously receive such candid feedback. What is even more impressive is how the participants have used the data. They have scheduled follow-up appointments to gain a deeper understanding of the feedback and to ask for guidance, advice, and formal mentoring.

This is a wonderful example of personal empowerment, taking responsibility for one's own development, and searching for opportunities to grow. They also sent a clear message to management: "Look over here! I am someone worth noticing and developing."

Consulting on this project has been so rewarding. I've become very attached to this group and to their leadership. What a refreshing approach. The leaders of this organization didn't say, "We'll tell you if we think you are high potential." They said, "You tell us, and show us, if you are."

These people are building a bridge to the future by taking advantage of every available learning opportunity, developing a broader understanding of the organization, and taking risks. In the process they are also building an incredible network of support and recognition throughout the organization.

Are You Working Without a Net?

Have you seen the disclaimer on television stunt shows, "Do not attempt this at home"? I think our careers should come with a warning like that: "Do not attempt any of this alone!"

We all need a net—a network. And to some degree we all have one. It's the people we know, professionally and personally, our contacts. I encourage you to inspect your net; you may find gaping holes and weak lines. Will your net hold?

This isn't an option! It is absolutely essential for women in the workplace. With a strong network of support, we are more effective in the present, more prepared for the future, and more of a resource to others. Effective networks connect us to people inside and outside the organization. These connections become conduits of information, insight, and support.

Your network is so much more than whom you know. It's also what you've done for them lately: how you have contributed to their success, added value to their organization, helped them achieve a goal, or connected them with someone they need to know.

Networking isn't passing out ten thousand business cards at a tradeshow. That's just an in-person version of spam. Networking is making a *real* connection—understanding what people care about and what they are trying to get done.

It is telling your story and asking others for theirs.

> Judy is a television producer in San Antonio, Texas, and one of the best networkers I know. She listens to people and works to understand what is important to them. Then she looks for ways to support their efforts. Judy becomes an extraordinary resource to the people in her network.
>
> She makes introductions, refers business, and shares knowledge. As busy as she is, she follows up and keeps in touch. More than anything else, she is deeply vested in the success of others—she pours herself into others with incred-

ible energy and authenticity. As a result, her relationships are rich and committed. Judy's net will definitely hold.

Here are seven ways to build your personal network. Which of these do you need to do or do more consistently?

1. *Take more social initiative.* Look for opportunities to meet people. Networking is not an event; it is a discipline.

2. *Join organizations of interest.* Get involved in industry and community associations. This means more than just showing up occasionally. Your network will only grow to the degree you get involved.

3. *Business cards are a must.* If your organization doesn't provide you with business cards, make the investment in yourself. Have them professionally made—this is not the time to scrimp with homemade, flimsy paper stock and cute clipart. And keep them with you always.

4. *Volunteer.* Sign up for causes that matter to you. You'll meet people who share your interests and concerns. Common ground is a great foundation to build on.

5. *Manage your contacts.* Instead of building a database, build a knowledge base. Go beyond collecting names and telephone numbers. Over time, if you pay attention and ask the right questions, you will learn the goals, interests, and challenges of your contacts. That's when they stop being contacts and become colleagues, friends, and resources.

6. *Add real value—find out what is important to your contacts.* When you see information that may be of value or interest, get it to them. When you meet someone they need to know, make the introduction.

7. *Keep in touch.* Send thank-you notes, birthday cards, and holiday greetings. Make opportunities to stay in front of your contacts in meaningful ways.

Most major industries have associations dedicated to the support and development of women in their field. In addition to the networks in your specific industry, these national organizations have a mission to promote professional women. Check for chapters in your area and get plugged into the network.

American Business Women's Association (ABWA)	www.abwahq.org	9100 Ward Pkwy. P. O. Box 8728 Kansas City, MO 64114-0728 800-228-0007
Business and Professional Women/USA (BPW/USA) Business and Profession Women's Foundation (BPW Foundation)	www.bpwusa.org	1900 M St., NW, Ste. 310 Washington, DC 20036 202-293-1100
National Association for Female Executives (NAFE)	www.nafe.com	60 E. 42nd St. Ste. 2700 New York, NY 10165 212-351-6400
National Association of Women Business Owners (NAWBO)	www.nawbo.org	8405 Greensboro Dr., Ste. 800 McLean, VA 22102 800-55-NAWBO
U.S. Women's Chamber of Commerce (USWCC)	www.uswcc.org	1200 G St., NW, Ste. 800 Washington, DC 20005 888-41-USWCC

Make an Appointment With Gratitude

With all of our technology—voice mail, e-mail, fax, and the beloved text messaging—handwritten thank-you notes may belong on the endangered list. It has been estimated that only 5 percent of business people in America actually take the time to sit down and write personal thank-you notes. We've become so high tech, we've lost touch with one of the most special and simple gestures of gratitude.

Every Friday afternoon I have a standing appointment with myself. I write five thank-you notes. I carry five stamped notes with me each week, so no matter where I am at the appointed time, I can honor this commitment. Quite often I find myself writing notes on the airplane, heading for home, thinking about the people who made the week possible and profitable, while reflecting on the relationships that make it all work.

I am learning that no matter how tired, discouraged, or overwhelmed I am, this exercise helps me find my balance. This commitment causes me to walk in the spirit of gratitude. I am also learning it is impossible to walk in the spirit of gratitude and be grumpy at the same time.

With this appointment in mind, I am always looking for and searching out people to appreciate. And I always find them.

Sometimes it's the skycap at an airport who helped me catch the last plane to somewhere, or the hotel employee who went out of her way to make sure everything was perfect for a conference. It might be my mom and dad, who pray for me every single day, or my husband who just makes me better.

It is never hard to find my five, and when finished with this exercise I am again reminded of how blessed I really am. More than once I've received this response from one of my thank-you notes: "You have no idea how much I needed that note right now." Then more than ever I am glad I kept my appointment with gratitude. Some appointments really are *divine*.

Elect Your Board of Directors

You use steel to sharpen steel, and one friend sharpens another.

—Proverbs 27:17

You are the CEO of your career, and you need a board of directors. These are people who long for and pray for your success. Your board might include personal, professional, and spiritual mentors—a group of people whom you trust and respect. They will encourage you and tell you the truth. They vest themselves in your success.

On my board of directors you will find people who have reached the level of success I aspire to, mentors who share their insight, visionaries who challenge me to think bigger, professionals in my field, business partners, and people who help me find my balance. Each of them adds perspective, and all of them make me better.

My parents are on the board. They hold a precious position there. They are my touchstone. My husband sits on the board as well. He is my home base and my shelter. The chairman of my board is Christ, without whom I can do nothing. When He endorses a project it is fully funded and richly blessed.

Your board is a resource and a commitment. These are the people you share your goals, action plans, ideas, and results with. When you aren't getting the results you need or when you feel "stuck," these are the people who can help you sort it out.

You may have two or ten people on your board. It may start small and grow over time. The important thing is to begin thinking about who should be on it and begin building it now.

Leverage the Power of Mentoring

On television medical dramas, you often see a swarm of interns following a doctor through hospital rounds. Stopping in each room, an intern will step forward, clear her throat, and provide the patient's case details. A nervous silence follows as the interns dare to diagnose and recommend treatment under the scrutinizing eye of the attending physician—the mentor.

Mentoring is an ancient practice, and I am absolutely passionate about it. The word *mentor* is of Greek origin, translated as "an experienced and trusted advisor." Who doesn't need one—or two or ten—of those?

Some of the most important lessons I have learned have come through mentoring. Without it I would not be where I am and, I dare say, who I am. My mentors have helped me center myself in difficult circumstances. They have challenged my perspective and shown me options I didn't see. They have inspired me, and more than once they believed in me more than I believed in myself.

Extensive research has been done around the promotability of women, and mentoring is a key success factor. It is far and away one of the most valuable strategies you can use to develop, promote, and center yourself. A good mentor, however, will not:

✓ Give you the answer or solve the problem for you

✓ Rescue you from yourself; big, bad bosses; and other corporate monsters

✓ Become professional parents

✓ Judge you

✓ Attempt to clone themselves in you

With that out of the way, I will tell you there are things you *can* and *should* expect from a good mentor. You can count on them to:

✓ Challenge you with tough, soul-searching questions

✓ Tell you the truth and help you confront the truth

✓ Encourage you to try new approaches

✓ Push you out of well-formed comfort zones

✓ Listen

✓ Offer new perspectives by challenging you to see old things in new ways

✓ Make recommendations and help you see options

✓ Help you learn from mistakes and celebrate successes

When you consider the barriers women face in the workplace, mentoring should be a top priority.

Get the Most Out of Mentoring

Realistically, you may have many mentors in your lifetime, and each of them will invest time, information, knowledge, understanding, and vision. You may have a situational mentor—someone you can run a specific scenario by to ask for input or advice. Other mentors may be skill based. They know how to do something you want to learn how to do or learn to do better. You may even have a high-level mentor. This is someone who can help you sort through your long-term goals and develop realistic plans of action.

Some mentors become lifelong friends, members of your extended family. Others won't, so be realistic in your expectations.

Many mentors or potential mentors may pass through your life, but there are characteristics to look for when choosing them. Look for mentors who:

✓ Possess a strong base of knowledge; they are respected and viewed as an expert in their field

✓ Have the highest personal standards

✓ Believe in mentoring—someone who is continually updating and upgrading their own skills

✓ Possess excellent interpersonal communication skills

✓ Will help you discover your own answers, not give you their answers

✓ You can trust because mentoring requires authenticity and honesty

The best mentoring is action oriented. It is not—I repeat—it is not doing lunch, commiserating over coffee, or amateur therapy. When mentoring works, it is protégé initiated and objective based. That means the mentor isn't chasing you down; you are chasing them down with real objectives.

Before asking someone to mentor you, here are some things to think about and prepare for:

✓ What you are hoping to learn—give your mentor something to work with

✓ Specific challenges you are facing

✓ Your performance objectives

✓ Projects you are working on

✓ Feedback you've received

✓ Where you want to be in one year, in five years, and in ten years

I encourage you to make mentoring a top priority. Think about what you want to learn, where you want to be in the future, and who candidates for your prospective mentors might be. Look inside and outside of the organization. There is no perfect formula—each mentoring relationship is unique.

You might even test a potential mentoring relationship with a specific scenario. Bring a challenge or an opportunity to someone you think may be a good mentor. Ask for their help in sorting it out. From the results you can decide if there's a good fit.

Brush the Dust Off Your Résumé

Where is your résumé?

I encourage you to find it, blow the dust off it, and bring it up-to-date. As you do that, understand the dynamics have changed. The résumé of the future will be a marketing brochure. Instead of presenting what you have done in the past, it will highlight the difference you made—the results you achieved in exciting and quantifiable terms.

In the past, résumés were primarily screening tools. Hiring managers would sort through a stack of résumés to arbitrarily decide which applicants would be invited to the next step. The new résumé is a marketing tool that highlights your strengths, quantifies your results, and projects future value.

Updating your résumé does not necessarily mean you are looking for a new job. In fact, you should consider a résumé update every six months. It should reflect the most current you. As you change and grow and achieve, it should evolve.

Put your marketing hat on and allow your résumé to sell your story!

Choices, Endings, and Beginnings

With all of this introspection and reflection, always remember, our most difficult circumstances can become powerful catalysts for change. Sometimes we have to become excruciatingly uncomfortable where we are before we are willing to consider and embrace a new opportunity.

What if you confirm what you've suspected for a while now? Perhaps you've wrestled with your choices—accept, change, or leave. You narrowed it down, and now you have made your final choice. You're in the wrong job. It's time to go.

When you're in pain, the natural reflex may be to cut and run, grabbing the first job opportunity as if it were a life preserver.

The last thing you may be thinking about is your long-term career plan. But here's the paradox: this is *exactly* the time to be thinking about it!

If that is where you find yourself now—you cannot accept your situation at work, and you have exhausted yourself trying to change it—there is a right way, and a wrong way, to go. Here are some important things to consider as you plan for job endings and new beginnings:

Before leaving the job you have, ask yourself accountable questions.

- ✓ Is it possible that you are getting in your own way?

- ✓ What feedback have you received, and how have you responded to it?

- ✓ How are you contributing to the problems you are experiencing?

- ✓ What have you tried?

- ✓ What should you try before deciding to go?

This is not intended to be an exercise in self-condemnation. It's quite the opposite, in fact. These are the questions that keep you from thinking like and believing you are powerless. It is reflecting on your personal accountability and empowerment.

Be careful not to take the problem with you when you go.

- ✓ It's quite possible to bring old baggage to new opportunities. If you are leaving a difficult situation, process those emotions thoroughly.

- ✓ Own the pieces that are yours.

- ✓ Learn what you can.

- ✓ Sort through the rubble and keep what makes you better.

✓ Leave the rest behind.

✓ Separate your endings from your beginnings so you don't pack disappointment and resentment with you.

There is no perfect job, and every "honeymoon" will end.

✓ All organizations have issues, and the grass really isn't greener over there. I can't count the number of times I've seen people jump ship and climb onto another boat, only to find they've moved from bad to "just as bad" or worse. Do your homework, manage your expectations, and hold out for the right opportunity.

You may have to move laterally to move forward, but rarely should you consider stepping backward.

✓ There may be times when a backward step makes sense. Just make sure your moves are strategic. Does the job you are considering take you closer to your long-term goals? If not, you are probably running from something and not running to something.

Never quit on the job.

✓ Have you ever met someone who has emotionally quit but keeps showing up at work? When you are disillusioned or disappointed, it may be easy to justify a lack of commitment. It will never be honorable. As long as you are picking up a paycheck, exchange it for real value. Anything less is unethical and kills your credibility.

✓ Knowing when it's time to go is important. How you leave and where you go matter, too.

Invest in Your Possibility—Release Your Potential

Building a bridge to the future is a personal investment. This is something women often fail to do for themselves. We let the pressures of the moment and the demands of the day block our vision of the future. If we allow that to happen, we may one day find ourselves stranded on the wrong side of our possibility.

You were designed for success. Don't settle for something less than that. Construct a big dream and back it up with a solid plan of action. Create a strong network of support, and leverage the power of mentoring. Manage your future as if it were the most important project of your career.

High-Impact Ideas

✓ Growth is imperative. You must be growing up or growing in the job you have. Staying where you are, as you are, is a prescription for becoming obsolete. All of us must build a bridge to the future.

✓ The time to prepare for your next opportunity is now. Once your company has posted an open position, it's probably too late. Get ahead of the curve by looking for and asking for experiences and exposures that will make you the top-of-mind, natural choice *before* a position opens.

✓ Look for opportunities to practice and demonstrate leadership. Two important things happen when you search out these experiences: you prepare for the future, and you send a message. The message reads, "Think of me when there is an opportunity."

✓ Developing a career plan begins with a great deal of personal reflection and a gap analysis—comparing where you are now with where you want to be in the future.

✓ When sketching your future, practice unlimited thinking. Don't worry in the beginning about *how* you will get there. Once you have defined your career objectives, you will isolate the gaps, develop action steps, anticipate obstacles, and identify the resources you need.

✓ With a strong network of support, we are more effective in the present, more prepared for the future, and more of a resource to others. Effective networks connect us to people inside and outside the organization. These connections become conduits of information, insight, and support.

✓ Make an appointment with gratitude.

✓ You are the CEO of your career, and you need a board of directors.

✓ Extensive research has been done around the promotability of women, and mentoring is a key success factor. It is far and away one of the most valuable strategies you can use to develop, promote, and center yourself. When you consider the barriers women face in the workplace, mentoring should be a top priority.

✓ The new résumé is a marketing tool that highlights your strengths, quantifies your results, and projects future value.

✓ The most difficult circumstances can become powerful catalysts for change. Sometimes we have to become excruciatingly uncomfortable before we are willing to consider and embrace a new opportunity.

✓ Knowing it is time to go is important. Where you go and how you leave matter, too.

✓ Manage your future as if it were the most important project of your career.

Questions for Reflection

If you could have any job, what would you choose and why?

_____

_____

_____

Is your network a database or a knowledge base?

_____

_____

_____

Who belongs on your board of directors?

_____

_____

_____

Action Items

Interview three successful people. Ask them to describe a challenging situation and what they did to overcome the obstacles.

"Test drive" a mentor. Choose a situation or challenge and run it by a potential mentor. This will give you an idea of the kind of mentor they might be.

Develop a rough sketch of your career plan. Share it with a mentor or a member of your board of directors. Ask for feedback.

Chapter 8

COMMANDMENT 7:
Think Like a Project Manager

IT'S VERY EASY to become task driven at work. Unless we are grounded by a plan, we can become reactive and shortsighted. When that happens, we end up looking more like short-order cooks, checking off the tasks and shouting, "Order up!" Even more discouraging is the real possibility of completing the tasks and falling short of the goal.

What would change about the way you manage your assignments if you thought of them as projects instead of tasks? How would your approach change if you started thinking more like a project manager?

Read this chapter with your work, your assignments—your *projects*—in mind. Look for ways to apply the following disciplines to what is already on your plate:

✓ Ask defining questions to create a clear picture of expected results.

✓ Speak more strategically, so people see you as a strategic thinker.

✓ Make confident decisions based on success criteria.

✓ Plan more effectively, so important pieces don't fall through the cracks.

✓ Monitor progress on the way to your goals.

✓ Keep people informed with relevant information.

✓ Manage expectations to avoid disappointment with results.

✓ Turn your stakeholders into shareholders.

✓ Anticipate and manage risk strategically.

✓ Imagine the ripple effect of your actions and your nonactions.

These behaviors are the hallmark of professionalism and effectiveness. As you apply the attributes of project management to your assignments, you are more compelling, confident, and prepared.

Project managers are fascinating. The good ones have an eclectic—almost paradoxical—set of skills. They must be tactical and strategic, task oriented and people oriented, marketers, planners, team builders, and communicators. We can learn a great deal from the disciplines of project management and apply these practices to our projects, assignments, and careers. We can even use project management success factors to measure effectiveness.

Project success has long been defined as on time, on budget, with high quality. Eric Verzuh in *The Fast Forward MBA in Project Management* gives us another perspective with five factors of success.[1] When you achieve these with your assignments, you have been successful.

1. Agreement on goals

2. A visible, measurable plan with clear accountabilities

3. Effective communication between everyone involved

4. A controlled scope—complete agreement on what the project includes and what it doesn't

5. Management endorsement and support

Knowing what makes a project successful is one thing. Knowing how to make that happen is another. The following strategies are about the how, beginning with how assignments are received.

Beware of Drive-by Delegation

Has this ever happened to you?

> You are innocently walking down the hallway or working intently. Out of nowhere your boss appears. She has just come from a meeting of some kind or another, and when she sees you, her eyes light up. You've seen that look before, but it's too late to run. You are about to receive an assignment. This is a drive-by delegation.
>
> While your boss is standing in front of you, the assignment makes perfect sense. You get it. The moment she moves away, you realize you do not have a clue what she wants you to do!

Here's where we can take a page from project management and a lesson from good project managers. It's called project definition, and it keeps you from flailing around in the dark. Here's how project definition works.[2]

The next time you receive an assignment, go back to your work area and make a list of what you know, or think you know, about this assignment. Write down every detail you can think of. Then review each item and make another list of questions you have. Make an appointment with your boss to review the specifics and clarify your questions.

Here are some answers you want to achieve through project definition:

✓ *What is the goal of this assignment?* What are we trying to accomplish? What is the picture of success? What does the end result look like? Make sure you and your boss have the same crystal-clear vision of the end result. There is nothing more disappointing than completing an assignment only to find out it isn't what your boss was looking for.

✓ *Why is this project important?* How does this assignment impact the priorities of the organization? Knowing this adds interest and inspiration to the work and allows you to work in context.

✓ *Where does this work connect with other work that is going on throughout the organization?* How does my project impact other initiatives, and how do they impact mine? If you don't understand these connections, you may duplicate work or create something others won't or can't use.

✓ *Who needs to be informed and updated?* Who are the stakeholders? How often would you like to receive updates? Whom will this assignment impact? Understanding whom your work impacts gives you important clues about how you will need to communicate.

✓ *When does the assignment need to be complete?* What are the significant milestones? Agreement up front on deadlines allows you to control your assignments and makes it less necessary for your boss to micromanage you.

If you set about *doing* before *defining,* your project will be more difficult, less supported, and ultimately less successful. Resist—with all of your might—the temptation to jump into action before you have carefully defined the assignment.

Understand What Drives Your Project

In every project there are drivers. Drivers limit or constrain projects, and project managers use them as decision-making guides. There are three drivers. All three may be important to your assignment, but only one of them is primary:

1. When time is the primary driver, there is an urgency to complete the project. Deadlines are driving you.

2. If money is primary, resources are limited. You must find ways to complete the assignment with a careful eye on costs.

3. Quality speaks to the elegance of a project. If quality comes first, you are less concerned with how long it takes or what it costs. You are more interested in adding value (i.e., adding functionality, making it easier to use, more unique, or harder for a competitor to duplicate).

A Broadway set designer put all of this into perspective for me with one simple question. When commissioned for a new theater set, he responds, "Do you want it fast, cheap, or beautiful? Pick two." This really works!

Think about it. If you want it fast and cheap, it won't be pretty! If you want it cheap and beautiful, it will take longer. And finally, if you want it beautiful and fast, it's going to be expensive.

Knowing what drives your project is important because it gives you a measurement for success, guides your decisions along the way, and helps you manage expectations. When you find yourself at a crossroads—choosing options or solving problems within the project—the driver will point you in the right direction.

✓ If time is pressing on your assignment, you will understand that meeting the deadline is more important than making it prettier or perfect. You may have a thousand creative ideas for making it better. You could get lost in the possibilities of this project, and if you do you will miss the mark.

✓ If money is the issue, you must look for ways to reduce costs and maximize resources. Using our set design as an example, this would mean understanding and focusing on basic requirements.

✓ If quality is the key success indicator, you are being measured on how special or effective the result is. Manage quality indicators carefully. Make sure everyone agrees in advance how quality will be measured.

I learned to see drivers more clearly through a lens of disappointment. On my own time, I developed a sales curriculum for the organization I worked for at the time. I spent weeks developing a gorgeous training manual. This thing was amazing!

When I proudly presented it to my boss, he flipped through it dismissively and said, "I am more interested in results than graphics. What will it cost to produce this for every sales representative?"

I was devastated. What a bad, bad boss.

In retrospect, I made a couple of big mistakes with that self-initiated project. I failed to understand what was most important to my boss—how he would measure success, what he considered quality.

I presented a training manual to him—a very, very beautiful training manual. But he wasn't interested in a manual. He wasn't in the market for an amazing layout with full-color graphics. He would have been very interested in the results achieved through the training, and that's what I needed to sell. When I didn't sell that quality, he evaluated my project on cost.

Be prepared. If you ask your boss what is most important—time, money, or quality—you are likely to hear, "All of the above." You'll probably need to dig down with some test questions to find out what is really driving your project. Ask questions like:

- ✓ If we found a way to make this really amazing, and it meant spending more money, would you want us to do that?

- ✓ If we had more time, we could make this even better. Can we have more time?

- ✓ We could save money if we eliminate this piece. Would you like to do that?

Once you've isolated the driver, realize it can move on you without your permission and without warning. What began as a quality-driven project can quickly become a schedule-driven project, and so on. You are wise to keep your finger on the pulse of your project and the people it will affect to detect even a subtle shift in what drives it.

Turn Your Stakeholders Into Shareholders

Stakeholders are the people who will be affected by your project. They may be the people using the process or report you create or the ones attending an event you coordinate. Your stakeholders may be internal or external customers who will use the product you design or the service you provide. Stakeholders generally have something to gain or lose as a result of your work.

Shareholders, on the other hand, are people who are vested in the project. Yes, like stakeholders, the results of the project will impact them, too. But shareholders have a sense of ownership, and ownership is created through involvement. The most successful project managers understand this dynamic, and they work very hard to involve the shareholders throughout the process of the project.

Once you have identified the stakeholders, identify ways to involve and vest them. Here are a few examples:

✓ Sharon was asked to develop a new employee orientation. She interviewed employees who had been with the company for less than one year to find out what would have made their introduction to the company more helpful. She also asked the corporate training team to advise her on developing a professional presentation. The finished project was welcomed by the employees, and the training team happily incorporated the changes into the corporate orientation process, knowing they had been included and allowed input throughout the project.

✓ Karen's assignment was to pilot a mentoring program for her company. She created an advisory board—a group of potential mentors and protégés to define the program requirements. This group met several times to create the strategy and develop a presentation to sell the concept. The credibility of the people Karen involved and the quality of their work were so impressive, senior management fully endorsed and funded the program.

✓ Pam was charged with developing corporate standards and best practices for hiring. She consulted with hiring managers throughout the organization to gain their perspective. When the procedures were drafted, she returned to the hiring managers and invited their feedback. When the procedures were rolled out, the changes were quickly embraced by the hiring managers.

In each of these cases, the stakeholders became part owners in the project. Instead of feeling like something was being done to them, they were treated as customers of the project and resources to it. The women in charge of these projects found ways to leverage internal strengths and create positive visibility for the people who would ultimately own the result.

Especially when your assignment introduces change, involvement will help you reduce resistance and increase cooperation. Some of the best advice I ever received is: "People act best on their own ideas." Or to put it another way: "People don't argue with their own data."

Break It Down, Make It Visible, and Keep Them Informed

Project managers know how to handle their own data. They are experts at breaking even their most complex project into tasks, actions, and deliverables. With outcomes firmly in mind, they identify the steps it will take to get there.

Think of your assignments like jigsaw puzzles and the tasks inside are the pieces. We set up the puzzle by spreading the pieces out on the table and turning them face up so we can look at them and figure out where they go.

The pieces must fit together to create the picture on the box. Some pieces go in first to create the framework, and we constantly refer to the picture on the box for clues about where pieces go. Missing pieces ruin the picture.

Managing the tasks of your assignment is like putting together a puzzle. The end result, or project goal, is the picture on the box. You have to keep that picture in front of you at all times—never losing sight of the desired outcome.

Begin by brainstorming all the tasks or pieces, and spread them out where you can see them. Project managers use sophisticated tools to break the project down. Or you can keep it simple by putting each task on a separate Post-it note or index card. Brainstorm everything that must be done to achieve the goal. For each task:

✓ Determine the time requirement.

✓ Decide how you will measure the success of this piece.

✓ Identify the risks and opportunities associated with this task: What could go right? What could go wrong? How will we know? When will we know?

✓ Determine who is responsible for completing this piece.

✓ Where does the piece fit into the puzzle?

You can answer that question by taking up another aspect of the project manager. They use a bevy of reports, graphs, and flowcharts to make a project's plan visible. They create confidence and build in accountability by ensuring everyone involved knows who is responsible for what.

When people understand what you are working on and the results you are driving toward, you invite confidence, respect, and support. When your plan is visible, you reduce miscommunications, misunderstandings, and missed expectations. It is also easier to imagine the ripple effect of your actions.

Look for ways to make your plans more accessible, more visible, and more meaningful to others. Use calendars, priority lists, and task updates to tell your story, keep everyone informed, and sell your plan.

Project managers carefully construct a communication plan. They use it to create focus, manage expectations, generate interest, maintain support, and market achievements. To be successful, your communication should consider:

✓ Who needs to know about what you are working on?

✓ What information is relevant and important to them?

✓ What is the right format or channel of communication?

✓ How often do people need to be updated?

In the context of your work, how well are you keeping your shareholders informed? Are you choosing the most effective channels of communication (i.e., formal, informal, in person, in writing, over the phone, and electronic)?

Many people feel overwhelmed with the amount of information they receive on a daily basis. How can you help your shareholders get to the information they need more efficiently?

You may want to ask for some feedback from your shareholders. Find out if they are getting the information they need from you or if they are receiving information that isn't useful. This will help you monitor your project from the shareholders' point of view.

Monitor Your Progress

At any given moment, project managers know exactly where the project is. They can tell you what is done, what isn't, and what must happen next to keep the project on track.

You can monitor your own progress the same way by understanding where you are at all times in relationship to your goals—by understanding what is on track, what isn't, and what needs to happen right now. When you have that kind of awareness, you build tremendous credibility, and you manage the most important project of all—the project called *you*.

A good example of monitoring your own progress is your performance review. You probably have this discussion at least once a year. Reviews typically include results you have achieved and areas for development and improvement. After you and your manager sign and date the review form, you should receive a copy. What do you do with that copy?

Many employees tell me they put it in a neat little file with other performance reviews and report cards they've collected through the years.

PUBLIC SERVICE ANNOUNCEMENT	*Your performance review is not a form to be completed, copied in triplicate, and filed away. It is a living document! Pull it out, mark it up, plan how you will address the developmental opportunities, and use it to monitor and market your progress.*

On a monthly or quarterly basis, bring your latest review to a meeting with your boss. Make it a document for discussion. Provide an update. Talk about how you are using the feedback, what you are learning, and the progress you've made. Talk about areas of concern, where you aren't making the progress you'd like to see, and ask for a recommendation.

When you do this, you are honoring and managing the feedback. You are building credibility and demonstrating the ability to manage yourself. You are also setting the stage for your next performance review by managing your boss's perceptions.

Be Strategic With Risk

In every project there is risk, and project managers are very strategic in how they manage it. You can plan for some risks, and others will surprise you—once. Identify risks to your goals by thinking about what could go wrong.

What could keep you from achieving your objectives? Find the risks hiding inside your work, and decide in advance how you will handle them if they do occur.

There are five things you can do with a risk:[3]

1. Accept risks that are unlikely or will have little impact on your goal. It probably won't happen, and even if it does, it won't make a huge difference.

2. Avoid significant risks by changing the scope. If the risk is significant and you can step completely around it by altering your plan, you may want to consider doing that.

3. Monitor your work and build in red flags that will alert you if something isn't happening on time or as planned. Have contingency plans in your pocket. When Plan A isn't working, shift decisively to Plan B.

4. Transfer or share the risk by building in guarantees, reimbursements, or fixed prices.

5. Mitigate the risk by working very hard to reduce its likelihood and the impact it will have on what you are trying to accomplish.

All of these decisions about risk have some things in common. It is assumed that you see risks that put your goals in peril, you understand these risks, and you know in advance how you will respond to them.

Put the Finishing Touches On

Closing a project is important, and good project managers know how to put the finishing touches on.

They understand that if you fail to close properly, you miss marvelous opportunities to market results, celebrate achievements, collect lessons learned, and recognize others.

The following are some of the devices project managers use to close the loop, with recommendations for how you might apply them to the work you do.

PROJECT MANAGERS...	YOU CAN...
Conduct a post-project review to compare actual results with the stated goals.	Schedule a meeting with your boss to review your goals and results. This is a marvelous way to market your efforts and achievements. It is also good for locating missed expectations and perception gaps.
Present results to project "shareholders" with a project summary report. They follow up with the people on whom the project had an impact.	Look for opportunities to follow up with the people on whom your work has an impact. Keep them up to date, in the loop, and informed.
Secure client acceptance by asking clients to sign off or approve deliverables and confirm acceptance.	Ask for feedback from your internal and external customers. Find out how satisfied they are with your work. Ensure their expectations are being met.
Lead postmortems to collect and document lessons learned.	Frequently ask, "What is going well? Why? What isn't? Why? What can we do differently to improve results?" When conducting a postmortem with others, it is important to hold the blame. This dialogue is to reinforce what works and learn from what doesn't. If it becomes an exercise in blaming, defending, or explaining, it won't bring real value. Begin postmortem meetings with clear ground rules to protect the purpose.
Reward and recognize people who contributed to success. Make projects rewarding experiences.	Send thank-you notes and brag about others. Look for ways to recognize, appreciate, and market the people who help you make it happen.
Hand off maintenance and detail unresolved issues with a project turnover memo to stakeholders.	Make quality handoffs so the balls don't drop as they leave your hands. Communicate outstanding issues and ensure those pieces don't fall through the cracks.

Look Strategic, Sound Strategic ... Every Day!

Thinking strategically is something women aren't generally known for. I know that's not necessarily fair, but it's true. If you want to create a reputation for being strategic, you must speak in strategic terms. In the guide *FYI: For Your Improvement,* authors Lombardo and Eichinger advise, "Every discipline has its lexicon. In order to be a member, you have to speak the code."[4]

Learn to speak strategically by becoming a student of strategy. Check out best-selling business books, pick up a copy of the *Harvard Business Review*, and study the strategies of successful business leaders. Learning this language is like learning any other language—immersing yourself in it is the best way to speak it fluently. You will find the language of strategy morphs. New words are created to describe emerging strategies or to put a fresh face on old ones.

First we had outsourcing, then offshoring, and now rightshoring. We had paradigms—and then shifts for those. We've used terms like *benchmarking, best practices*, and *organic growth*. I've heard organizations refer to walletshare, mindshare, and heartshare. There are value propositions and value migration, and by the time you read this, the language will have morphed again.

When we apply these disciplines, our work is suddenly more than a giant inbox of tasks and to dos. There is a strategy to the way we define, plan, manage, and, yes, even the way we communicate. We are more effective and more credible. We enjoy more recognition and support. Others have a greater sense of the value we create—and we have a greater sense of it, too.

Think like a project manager, and remember, the most important project you manage is *you*.

High-Impact Ideas

✓ Good project managers have an eclectic—almost paradoxical—set of skills. They are tactical and strategic, task oriented and people oriented, marketers, planners, team builders, and communicators.

✓ If you set about doing before defining, your project will be more difficult, less supported, and ultimately less successful. Resist—with all of your might—the temptation to jump into the action plan before you have carefully defined the assignment.

✓ In every project there are drivers. Drivers limit or constrain your project, and project managers use them to guide decisions. There are three drivers: time, money, and quality. All three may be important to your project, but only one of them is primary.

✓ Knowing what drives your project is essential, and drivers can shift on you without warning.

✓ Stakeholders are the people who will be affected by your project. Shareholders are people who are vested in it. They have a sense of ownership. Ownership is created through involvement. The most successful project managers understand this dynamic, and they work very hard to involve shareholders throughout the process of the project.

✓ When people understand what you are working on and the results you are driving, you invite confidence, respect, and support. When your plan is visible, you reduce miscommunications, misunderstandings, and missed expectations.

✓ Monitor your own progress like a project manager by understanding where you are at all times in relationship to your goals—by understanding what is on track, what isn't, and what needs to happen right now. When you have that kind of awareness, you build tremendous credibility, and you manage the most important project of all—the project called *you*.

✓ Managing the tasks of your assignment is like putting together a puzzle. The end result or project goal is the picture on the box. You have to keep that picture in front of you at all times—never losing sight of the desired outcome.

✓ Risk is inherent in every project, and there are five things you can do with it: accept, avoid, monitor, transfer, or mitigate it. Each of these decisions assumes that you see the risk, understand it, and know in advance how you will respond to it.

✓ Keep your project shareholders informed. A project communication plan is critical. Use it to create focus, generate interest, maintain support, and market your project.

✓ Use project management devices to close your loops. Look for opportunities to market results, celebrate achievements, collect lessons learned, and recognize others.

✓ You won't look strategic if you don't sound strategic.

Questions for Reflection

What would change if you treated your assignments like projects?

_____

_____

_____

Who are your stakeholders?

_____

_____

_____

How can you turn your stakeholders into shareholders?

_____

_____

_____

How can you put finishing touches on your project and close your loops?

_____

_____

_____

Action Items

Review a list of your current assignments. Which ones need more definition? Develop a list of questions you can ask to bring the project into focus.

Pull out your last performance review and use it to monitor your progress. How are you addressing the opportunities for improvement? Make an appointment with your boss to provide an update and discuss how you are using the feedback. Where you aren't making the progress you'd like to see, ask for input.

Review your work for risk. What could keep you from successfully achieving your goals? Determine in advance how you will respond to the risks you discover.

Chapter 9

COMMANDMENT 8:
Invest in the Success of Others

A **N AMAZING TRANSFORMATION** occurs when we lead others to the next level of performance or assist them in achieving their goals. They grow, we grow, and we create an amazing legacy. In this chapter you'll learn how to be an effective coach and mentor—how to develop skill, motivation, and commitment in others.

Coaching focuses on the current position, improving performance by developing job-specific knowledge and skills. Mentoring reaches into the future by developing the skills, knowledge, understanding, and connections that release potential and unlock possibility. Clearly, both are important, and occasionally they run in parallel. Even so, it's important to recognize the difference between the two and honor the purpose of each.

Regardless of whether you directly manage people or not, you have the opportunity—the obligation even—to coach and mentor others. I think you'll find it's in your own best interest to be a great coach, and mentoring is one of the most rewarding things you will ever do.

> Debra had been struggling for several months in her sales role. Normally a top producer, consistently exceeding every target, she found herself in a dry place. For ninety-nine

different reasons—most of which she doesn't personally control—her production dropped considerably. Her confidence fell with it.

Seeing how this difficult sales environment was impacting her, Debra's boss asked if she would be willing to coach several new employees as they came up to speed on the product line. Debra was happy to do it.

As she looks back on those frustrating months, the coaching assignment is the bright spot. "I was so discouraged with my production," she recalls. "When my boss asked me to be a coach, it was a vote of confidence at just the right the time. I was able to help the new sales associates come up to speed quickly. I made a real difference for those people. As I coached them, my confidence was restored. I know now that was the whole plan, and I'm grateful for a boss with that kind of insight." Bravo, boss!

Leave People Better Than You Found Them

As I write this chapter, one of the loveliest people I know is retiring. Her name is Frances, and she leaves behind a rich legacy. As she steps into the next season of her life, her work lives on in those she has developed, mentored, and encouraged along the way. She is so admired and respected, there isn't even the notion of replacing her. We know that cannot be done.

Surely the work will get done, but Frances can never be replaced.

Over the years, Frances became a resource for people within her organization, her field, and her community. Some of these people worked for her, and some worked with her. She reported to a few of them, and many of the people who benefited from her knowledge and experience now work for other organizations.

Frances was often asked for her advice and counsel because she is wise and trustworthy. People knew they could trust her with their ideas and challenges, even their humanness. She didn't bang people over the head with advice. Instead she helped people sort through the issues to discover options.

There are dozens of things that make Frances irreplaceable. But if there was only one thing I could point to—one attribute that defined her most—it would be this: she leaves everyone better than she found them.

That is my goal, too. My personal mission is to leave people a little better than I found them—a little more encouraged and optimistic about the future. A little more skilled. Feeling a little more valued, confident, and prepared for what is to come.

What I have learned from Frances, consulting with her on various projects through the years, is a gentle balance between the concern for people and the concern for results. She never sacrificed people for results, or results for people. She searched for ways to bring the best out in people, to achieve results. She invested herself fully in every project—especially the people projects. And she never lost sight of her core purpose and passion.

Frances invested in me, too. Many of my clients are referrals from her extensive network. I am the grateful beneficiary of her credibility and influence.

That is how Frances invested in others and built a bridge to the future. I smile when I think of the people who will cross that bridge—stepping surely into a new place with new possibilities.

Give All the Information Away

The most valuable, vital employees are rivers, not reservoirs, of information. They do not collect and store knowledge. They allow knowledge to flow through them by coaching and mentoring others. They give the information away.

That's too frightening for some. These people guard their knowledge, believing that being the only one to know gives them power and security. They withhold information and force people to pass through silly gates to get it. This reminds me of a troll on a bridge—those ugly creatures in storybooks that won't allow other characters to pass until they are thoroughly frightened and completely compliant—or, of course, until the troll is destroyed.

When I took the daunting step from a corporate position to consultant and speaker, one of the first calls I made was to Mark Sanborn, a best-selling author and speaker. He probably wouldn't remember this call, but I will never forget it. A colleague had suggested he might have some words of wisdom for me. Boldly, I left a message for Mr. Sanborn, and faithfully he returned the call.

For more than an hour, from an airport on a cell phone, he shared his knowledge of the industry with me. I took pages of notes, and my brain was on overload. The last question I asked Mr. Sanborn was, "Why would you give all of this to me? I am going to be your competitor, and I am going to be good at this! Doesn't that worry you?"

I will never forget what he said: "I'm not worried at all, because I can produce it faster than you can consume it. You are coming out of a world that thinks in terms of scarcity—where people compete for limited opportunities. I think in terms of abundance. There is more than enough to go around. My only requirement is, when someone comes to you asking for help, you give them everything you can."

I've tried very hard to keep that promise, and I have learned to think abundantly. Each time Mr. Sanborn publishes a book, I smile—as I purchase a copy—remembering his words: "I can produce it faster than you can consume it. Think abundantly, Dondi. Think abundantly."

That is when I learned that as you reach forward with one hand, you must reach back with the other. You bring people with you on this journey of success.

Find Someone to Mentor

As strongly as I have encouraged you to find a mentor, I also urge you to be one. It can be very difficult for women in the workplace to find female role models and mentors. You can step into that gap.

In the practice of mentoring, you add tremendous value. Organizations that have launched well-planned mentoring programs report lower employee turnover and higher productivity and employee satisfaction. They are more prepared in the marketplace because employees have a greater understanding of the business, customers, products, and services. Successful mentoring makes it more possible to:

- ✓ Attract and retain the best people

- ✓ Provide opportunities for career development

- ✓ Upgrade skills and knowledge

- ✓ Successfully transition employees into new roles and assignments

- ✓ Develop strong, capable leadership and a line of succession

- ✓ Pass on the intellectual legacy

- ✓ Connect people within the organization

- ✓ Improve the organization's scorecard

The benefits for the organization are compelling, and it doesn't stop there. Mentoring adds something to the people you invest yourself in, and it adds something to you. Without exception, in my work with mentoring programs, mentors report getting more out of the experience than they ever imagined.

Through mentoring you practice diagnosing situations and designing effective responses. You become more skilled in giving feedback and drawing out what is untapped potential. You experience the satisfaction of seeing someone reach higher and achieve more, and you build a reputation for growing people.

If your organization has a formal mentoring program, find out how to connect with that effort. If your organization doesn't have something in place, look for opportunities to mentor others right where you are.

Your mentoring may be real time and situational—helping a colleague or co-worker navigate a specific challenge or leverage an opportunity. It might be more developmental and longer term—equipping someone for the future and exploring possibilities. Or it may be mentoring a group of people who face a common challenge.

Several of the organizations I work with have discovered a real mentoring need for first-time team leaders and supervisors. Typically these people are promoted because they are really good at doing something. They are star performers. When they are promoted, a new reality hits: doing it is different than managing it. It is common for new supervisors to become discouraged in their new role. Without intervention we can actually set our stars up to fail.

This scenario is an excellent opportunity for group mentoring or coaching. These people have a common challenge, and they can learn a great deal with and from each other. Group coaching is a wonderful way to support people who are in a state of transition. And group mentoring is an effective strategy to prepare people for future transitions.

On more than one occasion, peer mentoring has been my strategy for groups at the highest levels of an organization. I've seen this kind of mentoring forge the team, open communication, and deepen the commitment team members have for each other.

> After completing a 360-degree feedback evaluation process, a senior management team gathered to receive their personal reports. Each report included data collected from a

self-evaluation and the evaluation of employees, peers, associates, and managers. The executives were asked to use the data to develop a personal development plan.

My role was to interpret the data for the entire management team and make recommendations for improvement at the group level. Instead of coming to the table with my answers, I decided to experiment with peer mentoring.

In small groups, I asked these executives to share one high score and one of their lower scores with their peers. The objective was to be a resource in the areas of strength, and to discuss action items in the areas of weakness. This was one of the most profound exercises I have ever witnessed.

To begin with, the executives held their reports close to the chest, nervous about revealing their personal data. As the session progressed, something changed. The reports were flung open, passed around, and openly discussed. I heard the language of mentoring all over the room: "Here's what that data may be telling you…" "Have you thought about…?" "What could you do to…?" "How can I…?" "What do you think this means?" People were out of their chairs, jumping into different discussions. The groups morphed from small to large and back again.

More came out of that session than action plans. This team came together. Trust was extended, tested, and strengthened. What began as anonymous communication became an honest, face-to-face dialogue. The managers felt supported and respected, validated and challenged. Many of those people continue to meet on a regular basis to share their progress and support each other. What a marvelous example of how mentoring impacts people on an individual and a group level.

When you begin looking for them, you will find mentoring opportunities all around you—inside and outside the organization. Consider:

✓ Partnering with your school district to mentor a child in your community

✓ Offering to mentor a new employee

✓ Teaching someone a skill you have mastered

✓ Delegating a challenging assignment to develop confidence, experience, and perspective

✓ Inviting another department to explore your processes

✓ Identifying a group of people who share a common challenge

✓ Giving a group of people across functional lines a problem to solve—a common goal

These are just a few examples of ways you can invest in the success of others through mentoring. I am confident you will also have many opportunities to improve performance through coaching and feedback.

Develop a Thinking People

The best coaching is not about fixing, solving, or answering. It is the process of helping another person discover their own answers. It is not about loaning your judgment. It is developing judgment in others.

When my son was in grade school, we lived in Colorado Springs. He came home from school one day announcing we had family homework to do.

Our assignment was to read an article and discuss it as a family. I didn't realize the article was designed to push every button in a mother's body! It was a newspaper story about a group of teenagers in the Northeast who were striking against their parents because their personal rights had been violated by a strict curfew. Are you kidding me?

We barely finished the article before I began preaching about these disrespectful, spoiled children who should be very grateful they didn't live in my house. A strict curfew would be the least of their human rights grievances.

When I finally ran out of steam, my son said, "All right. I guess we're finished with family homework." As he left the room, I knew I had really blown it. We hadn't discussed anything. I told. He listened. End of story.

I headed for my son's bedroom to apologize and then asked him to give me his opinion on the article. He was quiet for several excruciating minutes and then said, "I don't know. I guess what you said is probably right."

At that moment, I realized—in abject horror—my son didn't have an opinion because he'd not been allowed to have one! I became "Mom with a mission." I was determined to get my son an opinion.

Every day for the next three weeks I asked my son for his thoughts on pretty much everything: "What do you think?" "What would you do if...?" "How do you feel about...?" And for three very long weeks, my son responded with the same horrifying answer: "I don't know."

I will never forget where we were the day my son's opinion arrived. We were driving in the car when he said the beautiful words, "I think..." I nearly had to pull over! It was a wonderful moment. My son had an opinion. He could think for himself! And he hasn't stopped since.

That experience taught me something important: as long as we think for others, providing the answers and the solutions, there is absolutely no reason for them to learn how to think for themselves. We can actually teach people to rely on our judgment rather than to create their own judgment—and we rob them of the confidence that comes with it.

Do people ever come to you with questions and issues they should be able to handle independently? Of course they do. Be honest now. How do we often respond in those situations? We go into answer mode. We do it for them.

Why? Because, silly, it's faster and easier. And admit it, isn't there a little bit of ego in being the wise one with all the answers?

It may feel good to be the one with the answers. It is far more effective to be someone who helps people find their own answers. You can do this at work by:

✓ Asking questions to facilitate self-discovery

✓ Using hypothetical situations

✓ Teaching people to use you as a sounding board, not an encyclopedia or a procedures manual

One of the best practices in accelerated learning is never do for learners what they can do for themselves. Corporate trainers are encouraged to engage the brain and the body of adult learners by asking them to get up and do something. This is also a coaching key. Get people to think and do it for themselves.

Here's the last question in this series: Do you think they've figured this out? Of course they have. People are smart. They quickly figure out a way to get their work done. It's you.

It's been said, "If you are the only one who knows how to do it, you'll be doing it forever." That alone is motivation enough to develop the people around you! Here are eight strategies you can use to maximize your coaching opportunities:

1. *Let people find their own answers.* Instead of providing the answers or solving the problem for them, lead with questions to facilitate self-discovery: "What options do

you see?" "How would you like to handle this?" "How can we prevent this from happening again in the future?"

2. *Teach others how to diagnose issues.* Again, use questions as a primary coaching tool to assist others in identifying root causes: "What do you think is creating this issue?" "When did you first notice the problem?" "What have you tried so far?"

3. *When a problem is escalated to you for solving, work through resolution* with *them, not* for *them.* Demonstrate how you handle the situation. If this involves a customer, ask the other person to observe you. If appropriate, let them know next time it will be their turn to take the lead while you observe.

4. *Provide the why behind the what.* Sometimes people don't understand the real impact of their actions or nonactions. Make sure you make the connection between what you are asking for and why it matters. Help others work in context.

5. *Keep resistance low by using "I" language.* Instead of saying, "You need to…" say, "I need your help with…" Your language is like a giant finger pointing in someone's face. It invites a defensive response.

6. *Plan to follow up.* Make an appointment to ensure things are working the way they should, discuss progress, and debrief results. If you don't follow up, improvements may be temporary, and you may miss an opportunity to recognize success.

7. *Focus forward.* Leave people thinking about what they will do to improve, not what they failed to do in the past.

8. *Design meaningful experiences for practice.* Once you've isolated an area needing improvement, brainstorm ways to build practice into the work. This might include a special assignment, a project, or a problem to solve.

Master the Models of Feedback

We've talked a great deal about asking for and managing feedback. The other side of that process is giving feedback effectively. I learned a long time ago the old adage "We teach people how to treat us" is absolutely true. Can you think of someone in your life or work who needs retraining?

The way we format feedback or frame our messages is important. "Whole" messages allow us to take a stand, set appropriate boundaries, and achieve authentic commitment. The message we send has a better chance of being received and acted on.

There are four elements to a whole message:

1. *FACTS* What is happening?

2. *FEELINGS* How are you feeling about it?

3. *IMPACT* What is the impact on results, relationships, and stakeholders?

4. *COMMITMENT* What are you asking for?

Messages become contaminated when the elements are mislabeled.[1] In the following example, the facts don't sound like facts, they sound like judgment or blame: "You made a mistake on this report."

The first reaction to this feedback may be defensive. When people feel attacked, they tend to defend themselves—go figure!

Omitting one or more of the steps is like speaking in shorthand—asking others to read our minds and guess what we mean, what we feel, and what we want. We also risk missing the core issue and may fail to get a real and lasting commitment. When that happens, behaviors don't change for long, and we find ourselves returning again and again to address the problem.

Framed as a whole message, the above example sounds like this:

1. *FACTS* Many people rely on this data.

2. *FEELINGS* I am disappointed that we published a report with incorrect information.

3. *IMPACT* When that happens our group loses credibility.

4. *COMMITMENT* How can we ensure accuracy in the future?

This model takes a little practice, and it's worth the effort. I think you'll find using whole messages makes a real difference in the way people respond to your feedback.

Get Specific With Your Requests

When you are asking for a commitment, include the specifics: Whom are you asking? What are you asking for? When do you need it? Speak in context.

Instead of saying, "We need to prepare an agenda for tomorrow's meeting," include the specifics: "Martha, will you draft the agenda for tomorrow's meeting? I'd like to send it out by the end of business today. Once you've sketched it out, let's review it together before distributing it to the group."

You'll also want to avoid ambiguous words like "soon," "as soon as possible," and "right away." These words mean different things to different people. When you include specifics, you set people up for success. You can build on that momentum with balanced feedback.

Balance your feedback by looking for positives before you ask for changes or offer recommendations to improve. Go for a ratio of three to one—three positive observations for every change request. In the following example, we have an employee producing a daily report. Her work is the highest quality. The challenge is how long this project is taking every day.

> "Thank you for your attention to detail on this report. You are very thorough and precise, and I appreciate that. I am concerned, however, with the amount of time it takes to produce the report each day. What suggestions do you have for expediting the process without losing the quality?"

I like this model so much because it forces us to look for what is good and right in people before we focus on what needs to change. When giving feedback, sometimes the best approach is to start and stop with what is working. If your feedback is going to be unbalanced, err on the side of positive.

One form of positive feedback is recognition. It is one of the most powerful human motivators, and most of us probably don't use it nearly enough.

We all have the currency of recognition, and recognition is one of the most powerful ways to influence behavior. Regardless of whether or not you personally manage people, you can recognize them. Some research indicates that peer recognition can be more important to people than recognition from management.

Your recognition will have more impact if it is specific. Instead of saying, "Great job," tell that person what was great. Talk about the difference they made or the impact they had. Make sure all of this is authentic. I've never met anyone who was motivated or inspired by insincere praise.

Be a Motivating Force

Every year for my birthday, my husband takes me to SeaWorld to swim with the beluga whales. It is an awesome experience. I've learned more about the science and spirit of motivation in an hour there than from all the classes I've taken and books I've read on the subject combined.

The trainers at SeaWorld study the whales to discover what motivates each one. They look alike, but, like people, they are different. One is motivated by a giant red ball. Another wants to be tickled on her tummy—I'm telling you, she actually giggles. One just wants the trainer to dive in and play. Personal attention is what motivates him more than anything else.

For each whale, something different is the key, and the trainers find it to unlock the performance.

People are like whales in this way. Some are motivated by challenge, learning new skills, or solving a difficult problem. Others are inspired by making a real difference or by working in a group. Find out what motivates a person and you will have the key to unlock greater performance and deeper commitment. You will know how to draw out the best of who they are.

Pass It On

> As I was packing up to leave a change management seminar in Norfolk, Virginia, Leneicia, a senior manager, called me aside. We had been working through the strategies of introducing and implementing radical change in the workplace, and Leneicia said something quite profound: "My husband and I have been thinking about how the workplace has changed and will continue to change. What my daughter will need to succeed in this future place will be very different than what I needed."

This is big wisdom! To succeed in the future, her daughter *will* need a different set of skills and experiences. A summer job in a fast-food restaurant probably isn't going to prepare her for the workplace of tomorrow. Don't misunderstand. There is absolutely nothing wrong with a summer job in a fast-food restaurant, and there are important skills and disciplines we learn from those experiences. But Leneicia and her husband understand that won't be enough. Their daughter will need more.

She will need to be entrepreneurial, strategic, and analytical. She will need to speak more than one language and be exposed to international studies. Leadership skills will be paramount. And she will need powerful mentors and a strong network of support.

As Leneicia and her husband think this through, they understand there will be educational and experiential gaps to fill. This is the bridge they are building together—the investment they will make.

Look at your children and grandchildren. Imagine the workplace of their future. What will they need to thrive? How will you invest in their success?

High-Impact Ideas

✓ Regardless of whether you directly manage people or not, you have the opportunity—the obligation even—to coach and mentor others. It's in your own best interest to be a great coach, and mentoring is one of the most rewarding things you will ever do.

✓ Leave people better than you found them.

✓ The most valuable, vital employees are rivers, not reservoirs of information. They do not collect and store knowledge. They allow knowledge to flow through them by coaching and mentoring others. They give the information away.

✓ Think abundantly. There is more than enough success to go around.

✓ As you reach forward with one hand, you must reach back with the other. You bring people with you on this journey of success.

✓ Through mentoring you practice diagnosing situations and designing effective responses. You become more skilled in giving feedback and drawing out what is untapped potential. You experience the satisfaction of seeing someone reach higher and achieve more, and you build a reputation for growing people.

✓ The best coaching is not about fixing, solving, or answering. It is the process of helping another person discover their own answers. It is not about loaning your judgment. It is developing judgment in others.

✓ As long as we think for others, providing the answers and solutions, there is absolutely no reason for them to learn how to think for themselves. We can actually teach people to rely on our judgment rather than to create their own judgment—and we rob them of the confidence that comes with it.

✓ Teach people to use you as a sounding board, not an encyclopedia or a procedures manual.

✓ There are four pieces in a whole message: facts, feelings, impacts, and a request for commitment. If any of these elements are omitted, the message may alienate others, invite defensive responses, and fail to achieve real and lasting change.

✓ Balance your feedback by looking for positives before you ask for changes or offer recommendations to improve. Go for a ratio of three to one—three positive observations for every change request.

✓ Make recognition more meaningful by talking specifically about what was done and the difference it made.

✓ Find out what motivates people and you will have the key to unlock their performance and commitment. You will know how to draw out the best of who they are.

Questions for Reflection

Are you a reservoir or a river of knowledge?

_____

_____

_____

Who might benefit from your mentoring?

_____

_____

_____

How do you reward and recognize others?

_____

_____

_____

What could you do to make recognition more effective and more of a priority?

_____

_____

_____

Action Items

Investigate your organization's mentoring program. If there is one, find a way to get involved. If there isn't something in place, consider researching, developing, and proposing the idea.

Identify a feedback opportunity and practice making the message whole.

Make a list of the situations in which you are "doing for" others rather than "developing" others. Review the coaching tips and decide how you will handle these situations more effectively in the future.

Chapter 10

COMMANDMENT 9:
Break Through the Barriers

SMILE WHEN women innocently tell me, "I don't do politics." First I smile. Then I say, "Bunk."

| PUBLIC SERVICE ANNOUNCEMENT | *Every organization has politics. There is a game board and you're on it. You're either playing poorly or playing well. But you are most certainly playing.* |

The easiest and most reliable way for me to get a corporate groan is to ask any audience, anywhere, if their organization has any politics. Most organizations are steeped in politics, and that's not considered a good thing. It is possible—and should be considered mandatory—to play the political game effectively and with complete integrity.

Let's use a simple hypothetical situation to explore the game and the potential moves.

> Becky is very aware of the politics around her but isn't sure how to play. Her boss has selected a few favorites who seem to have a special set of rules. These people can do no wrong.

This inner circle eats lunch together almost every day, and they spend a great deal of time in conference, behind closed doors. Becky feels more like an outsider and an observer than a team member. She doesn't know how to get on the team—and frankly isn't sure she wants to.

Becky has a couple of problems here. She hasn't decided on the role she wants to play, and to this point she is centered on what others are doing, not doing, or being allowed to do. Those kinds of comparisons lead to battles that may not be worth losing, and they aren't the things she can personally control.

If Becky can shift her focus, she will take an important step. She needs to focus on the relationships she wants to create and the results she wants to achieve. She may need to professionally confront inequities that block her performance, and she is wise to ignore what doesn't impact her.

Those things may be unfair and irritating. They are also irrelevant. If I were Becky's mentor, I would ask her a few reflective questions—ten actually:

1. How do you want your relationships with others on the team to look?

2. What role do you want to play?

3. What strategies could you use to make your relationships and your role look more like that?

4. How do you add value to the team, and how are you communicating that value?

5. What would happen if you invited your boss or your co-workers to lunch?

6. If lunch isn't the issue, what do you want from the team?

7. How do the special rules for others impact you personally?

8. If there is a real impact, how can you professionally confront the problem?

9. If your efforts to change the situation fail, is this something you can accept?

10. If it doesn't change and you can't accept the situation, what options would you like to explore?

In some ways Becky's story reminds me of one Earl Nightingale told years ago.

> A retired couple moved south to enjoy their golden years in Florida. After just a few months, a moving van arrived. The couple had decided not to stay.
>
> A neighbor asked the husband why they were leaving. Were they not happy here?
>
> The husband sighed and told the neighbor they were leaving because his wife was so unhappy. She had made no friends. She had not been invited to the clubs and luncheons. She felt alone and wanted to go home where the people were friendly.
>
> As the moving van pulled away from the curb, the neighbor wondered: What had this stranger done to become less of a stranger? What had she done to reach out and initiate the relationships she wanted so much?
>
> The answer, of course, was...nothing.

I am not suggesting that Becky has done anything to deserve isolation within the team, or that her boss and co-workers aren't locking her out. My recommendation is for her to tightly focus on her objectives and not allow the sophomoric behaviors of anyone to keep her from feeling powerful, effective, and valued. Becky is not a victim, and I would urge her not to begin thinking or behaving like one.

The Red-faced Woman: A Lesson About Motives

I knew a storm was approaching as I saw a woman maneuvering (marching actually) through the crowd at a conference on the East Coast. Her face was turning red, and she was making a beeline right for me. This one reads like the script from a play. I hope you enjoy the show. (I did.)

RED-FACED WOMAN. You do not understand corporate politics at all.

DONDI, *taking a deep breath and praying for poise.* That's interesting feedback. Why do you say that?

RED-FACED WOMAN. My boss is the president's daughter, and nothing you said here will work on *her.*

DONDI, *smiling sweetly, as one eyebrow involuntarily climbs up my forehead.* What are you trying to do to her?

RED-FACED WOMAN, *enunciating each of these words very clearly, while her faces gets redder.* Don't you get it? She is the *president's daughter!*

DONDI. What about being the president's daughter poses a problem for you?

RED-FACED WOMAN. She gets away with everything! She is totally incompetent and she gets away with it! Everyone knows it, but no one can do anything about it because *she is the president's daughter!*

DONDI. How can you help her? (*Now I was having a really good time conducting research on how red a face can get.*)

RED-FACED WOMAN, *nearly screaming now in exasperation.* It's not my job to help her!

DONDI, *still smiling, teeth maybe grinding just a little.* What is your job?

RED-FACED WOMAN. My job is to produce statistical reports.

DONDI. Can you help your boss by the way you do your job? Can you make her look good, perhaps more competent? (*I honestly did not know a face could get this red. It was amazing.*)

RED-FACED WOMAN. I don't want to make her look good!

DONDI. What do you want? (*Now she was wearing me out.*)

RED-FACED WOMAN. I want her to be held accountable!

DONDI, *who is really over it now.* No, you want her to look bad. You want her to be properly punished. How will that help you be more effective? What do you gain by her loss?

That's when she stomped off with her bright-red face.

You get the point. This woman wasn't interested in becoming more effective at work. Her goal was to expose the weakness of another person, and nothing of value will ever come from a bad motive.

Having said that, can you relate to the red-faced woman and her frustration? I can.

The questions I asked her really weren't intended to send her stomping away. They were inviting her to reassess the situation and focus on a goal more worthy of her attention. That's an important lesson in the game of politics. Make sure what you are working for is something you can be proud of.

Send an Invitation to Your Partners to Play—Nicely

Have you ever received an instant message on your computer inviting you to play a game online? You are given the opportunity to accept the invitation or decline it. I receive these invitations from my husband inviting me to play Scrabble or UNO online. This may happen when I'm in a hotel far away from home or when he is in the next room. I think this is very sweet, and I usually accept.

Directly and indirectly we send messages to our business partners: "Do you want to play?" and "How do you want to play?" Our invitations signal people to collaborate or compete, defend or block. Many of the commandments we've discussed so far will help you play the political game with integrity and confidence.

✓ What you believe about yourself and others will shape the strategy of the game.

✓ Not all of the rules are written on the box. Some are assumed, unspoken, and unpublished.

✓ There are masters, mentors, of the game—people who have learned to play very well. These people are valuable resources because they understand the subtle nuances.

✓ The game is challenging. It's supposed to be.

✓ Increasing your awareness of what others need and what they are trying to accomplish allows you to position yourself as a partner in the game.

✓ When you understand the organization and the situation, you can move with more confidence.

✓ Anticipating how your moves will impact others is important.

✓ Turning conflict into collaboration and negotiating effectively makes it more possible to create winners without creating losers.

✓ Playing passively, aggressively, or emotionally is not the best strategy.

✓ A strong network is a definite advantage.

✓ Sometimes helping another win is your win.

✓ Not everyone in the game will play fair, and sometimes the deck is stacked against you. If you focus on or whine about these inequities, you will play with less credibility and power.

✓ You always have choices and options in the game. Make those choices and exercise your options with your objectives firmly in mind.

✓ The level of play depends on the standards you create. When you raise the standard of play, you invite others to step up, too.

✓ Teaching others to play effectively makes the game more rewarding for everyone.

✓ You will be remembered most by how you played the game.

The whole idea of politics can be distasteful until we see it as a game of strategy—a game that can be played ethically, purposefully, and effectively. Once you make that mental shift, you will engage differently.

The Border Problem at Work

All organizations have politics, and they all have invisible borders and boundaries. If you want to see where the lines are drawn, pull out the organizational chart.

Each department and division has a purpose, objectives, and standards of performance. Across the lines of an organization it's possible, and common, for objectives to conflict. One department may be charged with production. Another is responsible for quality. One group is expected to take risk. Another is responsible for controlling it. What begins as a system of checks and balances can quickly become us vs. them.

When that happens we begin to view our partners as enemies— a necessary evil down the hall. We spend our time and energy defending ourselves, blaming them, and documenting everything. I've seen organizations so caught up in this kind of weird dysfunction that they forgot the real mission!

In the book *Silos, Politics, and Turf Wars,* one of my favorite authors, Patrick Lencioni, makes a profound discovery. You destroy the barriers and topple the silos by binding people across the organization to a common objective.[1]

In addition to the normal operating objectives like revenue, quality, and profitability, people must have a shared objective. You find that objective by asking: What is the most important thing we should all be focusing on in the next thirty, sixty, or ninety days? What is the one thing that will make the greatest difference to this organization? How does each of us impact that one thing?

It would be wonderful if your organization made the commitment to break through departmental barriers. Your job would be easier and you would enjoy it more. You would spend less time documenting and more time producing. Yes, that would be awesome. Realistically, this is probably one of those it-begins-with-you situations. You can't wait for the organization to figure this out. And the good news? You don't have to.

You can partner more effectively now. You can be a more valuable team player today. You can make that decision and that difference.

Partnering across the borders of your organization comes with a set of rules. If these rules are broken, partnerships suffer, trust is broken, and you have to start over—go directly to jail, do not pass go, do not collect $200.

Twelve Rules of Engagement

1. Find your empathy. Demonstrate a sincere willingness to try to understand your partners. Go out of your way to understand their processes and what they need from you to play nicely.

2. Build on the foundation of common ground. Remember you are on the same team here. Your partners are not the enemy.

3. Use positive communications. Talk about what you want, what you are, and what you can do.

4. Trust has always been, and will always be, built in the details. Follow up and follow through. Keep promises, and return every phone call the same day—even if you don't have the answer, and especially when it's ugly. The second you realize you can't keep a commitment—for whatever reason—let your partners know. See rule 5.

5. Use the right channel of communication. Choose the channel based on your objective.[2] If you just want to update your partners, go ahead and do that in writing. Never use e-mail or voice mail—especially after they've gone home for the day—to avoid having a real, or difficult, conversation. Some things don't belong in writing and should never be written. That's what car keys, legs, backbones, and voices are for, to bring you face-to-face.

6. Eliminate all back channel communications. This is talking about your business partners instead of to them. See rule 7.

7. Never, ever throw a business partner under the bus—even when they richly deserve it—by blaming them for something that did or didn't happen. That's a discussion you have with partners in private. Publicly, especially in front of customers, you stand next to your partner, swallow the bitter pill, and take the heat.

8. Make it a top priority to appreciate and recognize partners. Make them look good. That's a currency that creates influence.

9. The cavalry is not coming. Not ever. Move on. Processes and people will never be perfect. There is no one coming on a white horse to magically fix the problems that plague you. See rules 1, 2, 5, 6, 7, 11, and 12.

10. Use partnering words like *we* and *ours*.

11. When things start to slide sideways, communicate more! Turn up the reception and frequency, not the volume.

12. Before hitting send on that fireball of an e-mail you just hammered out, ask yourself a few questions: What is my real motive? Is my goal to fix the problem or fix the blame? What is the business objective? Is this a rant or a solution? Will this message build trust or destroy it? Will this invite cooperation or resistance? And do I really need to send a carbon copy to the universe?

Break through the barriers within your organization by isolating and evaluating them objectively. See them as problems to solve, and call on your awareness and creativity. Empower yourself by managing your focus. Remain objective based in your responses and don't allow yourself to be distracted by what is trivial or juvenile—those issues are not worthy of your attention.

Build relationships behind the enemy lines. Turn your adversaries into allies by understanding their needs and declaring your intention to be a valuable partner. Confront what needs confronting professionally and assertively. Teach your partners how to do business with you. Negotiate for what you need, and find ways to invest in the success of your partners.

Breaking through the barriers positions you to increase your value to the organization and to create new opportunities for yourself.

High-Impact Ideas

✓ Every organization has politics. There is a game board, and you're on it. You're either playing poorly or playing well, but you are most certainly playing.

✓ Directly and indirectly we send messages to our business partners: "Do you want to play?" and "How do you want to play?" Our invitations signal people to collaborate or compete, defend or block.

✓ Many of the strategies we've discussed so far will help you play the political game with integrity and confidence.

✓ Nothing of value will ever come from a bad motive. Make sure what you are working for is something you can be proud of.

✓ The whole idea of politics can be distasteful until we see it as a game of strategy—a game that can be played ethically, purposefully, and effectively. Once you make that mental shift, you will engage differently.

✓ Each department and division has a purpose, objectives, and standards of performance. Across the lines of an organization it's possible, and common, for objectives to conflict.

✓ You can partner more effectively now. You can be a more valuable team player today. You can make that decision and that difference.

✓ Where there are barriers, find the common ground and common goals.

✓ Use the rules of engagement to partner across organizational boundaries.

✓ Break through the barriers within your organization by isolating and evaluating them objectively. See them as problems to solve, and call on your awareness and creativity.

Questions for Reflection

What would change if you viewed organizational politics as a game of strategy that can be played with integrity?

_____

_____

_____

How can you send an invitation to partner with people across organizational lines?

_____

_____

_____

Where do you need to repair a relationship in order to play more effectively?

_____

_____

_____

Action Items

If you are struggling to find your balance inside a politically charged situation, review your notes on negotiation. How would a master negotiator approach your problem?

Make an appointment with someone in another department—someone you are having difficulty partnering with. There are only two objectives for this meeting: (1) to understand your partner's process better, and (2) to find out what you can do to be a better partner. Stick to your agenda, even if there are 149 things you need them to do differently.

Review the rules of engagement. Which ones are you practicing consistently? Which ones need a greater commitment from you?

Ask a mentor to review the rules of engagement with you. Based on her experience, what rules would she add to the list?

Chapter 11

COMMANDMENT 10:
Add Value to Everything You Do

REMEMBER THE DAY you applied for the job you have now? Remember practicing for your interview and planning what to wear? Remember how nervous you were? Remember thinking and praying, "Pick me! Please pick me!"

And they did. They picked you! Months or even years later, are you still thinking, "I'm so glad they picked me"?

Sometimes we need to fall in love with our jobs again—to remember what we love about them and why we do what we do. One of the best ways to do that is to remember the day they picked you and look for ways to add value to every task, every assignment, and every communication. As you read this chapter, I hope you will search for and discover how you can become more valuable, because opportunity always follows value.

Are you looking for job security? Get over it.

PUBLIC SERVICE ANNOUNCEMENT	*There is no such thing as job security, so stop looking for it.*

In years past, employers were almost parental. As long as you did a good job, your employer would look after you with a paycheck, benefits, and a company picnic. Those days are gone.

Employers don't want to be parents. And even if you do a great job, there really are no guarantees. This shift in the workplace has left many employees feeling like orphans—disillusioned and tentative about taking risks and standing out. That is not the right answer!

The way to secure your future is to become more valuable—more vital. Now for the really good news: you get to decide how valuable and vital you want to be.

Increase Your Value to Create Your Opportunity

You are an asset to your organization. You have real value. When you increase your value, you create opportunity. (This has to work. It's the law of sowing and reaping, and it will work for you.)

On page 222 is a model used in consultative sales and relationship management strategies. I've adapted it for our use to illustrate how you add value to create your own opportunity.

At the base of the pyramid you are a *commodity*—nothing more or less. You come in, meet some minimum requirements, collect a paycheck, and go home. There is nothing special or distinguishing about the way you work.

As a commodity you are simply completing assignments with a set of technical skills. Here you are very easy to replace. You won't be surprised to learn this is where you will find the lowest job satisfaction, the most negativity, and the highest absenteeism. When layoffs happen, these are the first people to go.

Women don't grow up dreaming about being a commodity. We dream about being presidents, teachers, scientists, and astronauts. We dream about changing the world. How then do so many of us end up in the commodity zone?

The commodity people I meet didn't plan or purpose to be here. Some of them didn't get the recognition, the raise, or the promotion they believed they deserved. Others become weary of beating their heads against walls of bureaucracy, cutting through endless red tape, or dancing around the politics. Often they work for ineffective leaders who discourage initiative and creativity. They stopped growing and developing, and the work became drudgery.

They forgot their dream and how to dream. They know what to do, and maybe even how to do it well, but they forgot *why* they do it. There is no purpose in it for them.

Somewhere along the way, commodity people stopped trying to change the world, and they settled into a robotic punching of the clock. Many of them have retired in place and quit on the job.

If that describes you, I encourage you to begin again. Today, right where you are, in the job you have, find a way to increase your value. Do that tomorrow, too. Do it every day for week. You were not designed to be a commodity. Your opportunity is calling!

Put a Little Topspin on the Ball

You begin to pull away from the crowd when you look for ways to *add value.* This is where you push beyond base expectations. You add creativity and commitment to your technical skills to put a little topspin on the ball.

If your boss asks you to gather data for an important presentation, you add value by getting the information you were asked for and considering what else your boss may need to be more fully prepared. Who will be in this meeting? What questions or concerns might they have? You bring the data…and more.

Adding value is the way you appear, prepare, and organize. It can be found in your presentation, your execution, and your follow-through. It is demonstrated in how you understand the needs and exceed the expectations of your customers.

Who Are Your Customers Anyway?

To add real value you may need to rethink who your customers are. Your customers may be external—the people who buy or use your products and services. But you also have internal customers—the people who report to you, peers, associates, and your boss. What would change if you began to see and treat all of these people like your most valuable customers? What would change about the way you work if you found the answers to these questions?

✓ Who are my customers?

✓ What do my customers need?

✓ How can I become a greater resource to them?

✓ How can I make my customers more successful?

✓ How can I be more responsive?

✓ How can I anticipate their needs and be more proactive in addressing them?

You create extreme loyalty, credibility, and influence with customers when you demonstrate a solid understanding of their challenges, needs, and expectations. The perception your customers have of your service is entirely based on that awareness.

If you meet expectations, your service is perceived as satisfactory. If you don't, the service was disappointing. Your service is considered exceptional only when you consistently exceed the expectations of your customers—when you add value.

Make It Easier for People to Do Business With You

At the *user-friendly* level, you make it easier for people to do business with you. You are building a strong professional network and becoming a greater resource to more people.

We've all encountered people at work who are not easy to do business with. They may be very knowledgeable, but they also are resistant and grumpy, unavailable and unapproachable. At some point we look for ways to work around them, and that's when they become less essential to the mission. Less essential is just another way of saying less valuable.

Lisa is a human resources representative, charged with managing the annual employee benefits enrollment. Each year she sends out hundreds of employee selection packages. To confirm the packages have been received and the selection deadline is clear, employees are asked to sign and return a confirmation receipt.

In years past, less than 20 percent of the employees confirmed receipt with the initial request. Lisa would spend hours following up with reminders and multiple requests—harping on employees to sign and return the form. Then she asked herself the user-friendly question: "How can I make this step easier for my customers?"

She did a little customer research and tested a few options. Ultimately she decided on an electronic receipt. One week after the benefits packages were distributed, Lisa sent an e-mail to every employee in the organization. In this message, her customers were reminded to look for the package and make a note of the selection deadline. They were also given contact information for questions or to locate a missing package. When the message was opened, an automatic e-mail receipt was generated for Lisa's tracking purposes.

Her solution was successful.

Instead of trying to increase compliance with her process, Lisa viewed the process from her customers' perspective and found a way to make it more user-friendly. When she stopped policing her process, she found a way to improve it.

Bring Solutions to the Table

Next, you become more valuable to the organization when you search for and deliver *solutions*. At this level you are not waiting for an assignment. You are actively engaged in the process of continuous improvement. Here you are looking for:

✓ What costs too much?

✓ What takes too long?

✓ What is poor in quality?

✓ What falls through the cracks?

✓ What is outdated, inefficient, or ineffective?

✓ Where are we missing an opportunity?

Some problems you can solve on your own. When you do, find a way to market your results in quantifiable terms. When you save the company time or money, find a way to tell that story!

Sometimes you can't solve the problem on your own. In those cases you'll need to sell your solutions to others. That means doing your homework and presenting your ideas in a compelling way. Here your goal is to influence the people who can give your ideas legs to run on.

Help Your Organization Anticipate the Future

At the peak of the pyramid you help your organization anticipate and prepare for the future. You think long-term and strategically. You have internalized the vision. You ask questions and seek to understand:

✓ What will our customers or shareholders need and expect from us five years from now?

✓ What trends will impact our products and services?

✓ Who will our competitors be?

✓ What opportunities must we be prepared to maximize?

✓ What threats will we encounter?

✓ What could derail us and keep us from realizing our vision?

✓ What are other organizations like ours doing to prepare for the future?

✓ What could we learn from other industries or disciplines?

An amazing thing happens when you reflect on questions like this. The answers will come. You will see and hear things you may not have noticed before—an article in the newspaper, an advertisement in a magazine, or a comment from a customer. If you keep asking the strategic questions, the answers will arrive, and this is not a coincidence. The answers were always there. You just weren't looking for them.

Search for Best Practices

My work in talent management and mentoring programs exposes me to many industries and fields. I find common challenges and meet the most innovative people. Together we search for effective ways to identify and develop leadership. We look for best practices. What I learn from my experience with one organization can be of tremendous value for another.

Over time we have created a community, a network of professionals who share what they are learning. We have built a bank of best practices. The bank is a way for people to deposit and withdraw ideas, showcase their successes, and openly discuss their challenges. The currency is innovation, and I have the distinct pleasure of being a best-practices broker.

You can broker best practices, too. Help your organization anticipate the future by stepping out of your industry to compare processes and search for best practices in other fields. Build a broad network of contacts and make it a goal to learn from them:

✓ What do they see on the horizon?

✓ What are they doing to prepare for it?

✓ Even though you work in different fields, what common challenges do you face?

✓ What processes do you have in common?

✓ How are they addressing the challenges?

This is a wonderful way to network. People enjoy talking about what they are learning and producing. And you may have the answer they have been searching for. When that happens, you become a contributor in their success.

Find Yourself and Stretch Yourself

Where do you see yourself on the Value Pyramid now? Wherever that may be, what can you do to reach for the next level of value?

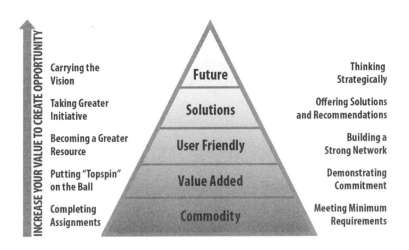

If you are feeling like a commodity at work, this isn't a message telling you to fall on your sword or pack up your toys and go home. It is your call to action. I don't think this process is necessarily

linear. You may find ways to add value and create solutions simultaneously.

While it's not linear, I believe it would be very difficult to move
from the commodity level to anticipating the future overnight.
You build credibility, influence, and a deep understanding of your
customers at the levels below that. Once that foundation is firmly
in place, you will have the currency you need to make a real impact
on the future.

Resolve to begin where you are and look for ways to operate
more fully at other levels of value. The very moment you decide to
increase your value, the process has already begun.

The truth of this model was a painful, eye-opening reality for
Carolyn. I met her at a conference, and I'll never forget her. She
could not hold back tears as she told her story.

About a year before, Carolyn had accepted a new job. In the beginning she was so excited with the opportunity. She couldn't work hard
enough, stay late enough, come in early enough, or volunteer enough.

Some of her expectations of the job weren't met. At first she was
able to overlook these disappointments. But as time went on resentment crept in. She stopped coming in early and working late. She
quit volunteering for special projects.

She withdrew her value.

She finished her story with these words: "I'm at this conference to
save my job. I am now considered a performance problem, and this
workshop is part of my performance improvement plan."

PUBLIC SERVICE ANNOUNCEMENT	*You will never, ever, ever—regardless of how you justify or rationalize your disillusionment—create more opportunity for yourself by depreciating in value!*

Sometimes opportunity doesn't arrive as quickly as you'd like.
It may not even come to you where you work now. But when you

add value, opportunity absolutely, positively will show up. It's a rule! What you sow, you will reap.

Are you disappointed with your job, your boss, or the organization you work for? Have you been making value withdrawals? Stop it!

By the way, when it matters the most, you won't feel like practicing anything you've learned here. That's why they call it discipline, and that's why doing it sets you apart—the average person won't.

Something else happens when you apply this model. You will enjoy your job more! You will feel more empowered, engaged, and motivated. You don't rely on other people to pull commitment out of you. Your commitment comes from a place inside of yourself.

You are no longer worried about job security. You know that isn't something your employer can promise. Your confidence comes from the value you bring and the difference you make.

High-Impact Ideas

✓ One of the best ways to fall in love with your work again is to remember the day they picked you and look for ways to add value to every task, every assignment, and every communication.

✓ Opportunity always follows value.

✓ There is no such thing as job security. The only way to secure the future is to become more valuable—more vital. You get to decide how valuable and vital you want to be.

✓ You are an asset to your organization. When you increase your value, you create opportunity.

✓ At the base of the pyramid you are a *commodity*—nothing more or less. You come in, meet some minimum requirements, collect a paycheck, and go home. There is nothing special or distinguishing about the way you work.

✓ Adding value is the way you appear, prepare, and organize. It can be found in your presentation and in your execution. It is how you understand the needs and exceed the expectations of your customers.

✓ At the *user-friendly* level, you make it easier for people to do business with you. You are building a strong professional network and becoming a greater resource to more people.

✓ Instead of trying to increase compliance with your processes, view them from your customer's perspective and find ways to make them more user-friendly.

✓ You become more valuable to the organization when you search for and deliver *solutions*. At this level you are not waiting for an assignment. You are actively engaged in the process of continuous improvement.

✓ At the peak of the pyramid, you help your organization anticipate and prepare for the future. You think long-term and strategically. You own the vision. You ask questions and seek to understand.

✓ Look outside of your industry or field to compare processes and locate best practices.

✓ You will never, ever, ever—regardless of how you justify or rationalize your disillusionment—create more opportunity for yourself by depreciating in value!

✓ When it matters the most, you won't feel like practicing anything you've learned here. That's why they call it discipline, and that's why doing it sets you apart—the average person won't.

Questions for Reflection

Are you appreciating or depreciating as an asset to the organization?

_____

_____

_____

Where do you see yourself on the Value Pyramid model?

_____

_____

_____

What can you do to operate more fully at a higher level?

_____

_____

_____

What would change about your approach if you assume there is a way to add value to every task and project?

_____

_____

_____

Who are your customers?

_____

_____

_____

How can you exceed your customers' expectations?

_____

_____

_____

Where are you trying to enforce your process and make people comply?

_____

_____

_____

How can you build commitment to the process by making it user-friendly?

_____

_____

_____

Action Items

Discuss the value model with a mentor. Brainstorm ways you can increase your value to create opportunity.

Identify at least three ways you can make it easier for people to do business with you.

Analyze a business problem and present a solution to your boss.

Interview your customers to understand their expectations better and learn how you can add value.

Chapter 12

Answering the Call

Using a dull ax requires great strength, so sharpen the blade.
That's the value of wisdom; it helps you succeed.
—Ecclesiastes 10:10, NLT

I **HAVE ALWAYS** been a collector of ideas, tools, and tactics—reading ferociously—being inspired and challenged by new approaches and best practices. Before I could afford to, I began building a library of business books and professional journals.

My favorite retreat is still the bookstore. Some of my best mentors have met with me in the pages of a book. Unlike some of my favorite women, I think one *can* have too many shoes, but it would be very difficult to have too many books or too many ideas. Over the years, the collection of titles and authors has grown considerably, and I have learned that collecting ideas isn't enough. You must use them.

Sometimes as I look over an audience of seasoned professionals, I make a confession: "This isn't all new. It's likely, even probable, that you will hear some things you've heard before, presented in a new way, or with new application." Sometimes the best ideas are timeless and the most profound concepts are surprisingly simple.

The point isn't: Do you know this stuff? The point is: Are you really doing it? Are you applying what you know and practicing what you have learned?

The same is true with potential. Potential is worthless until it is released and realized. I've met plenty of people with extraordinary potential who will never amount to anything of real value. They lack discipline, resiliency, and consistency. They give up too easily and aren't willing to pay the price. It's frustrating to work with people like that because, at some point, you realize you want something for them more than they want it for themselves.

A worthwhile goal will always cost you something. It will stretch you. If it doesn't, it's not a goal—it's just another nice idea in your collection.

In the end it really isn't about what you know. It's about what you do. By now I hope you've isolated what you will do to put these ideas to work. These choices and steps are very personal and they accumulate—they become who you are and what you are known for.

You Are Building a Brand

Branding is a marketing strategy once reserved for large companies to promote and sell. A brand does just what it implies. It imprints an image on the brain; it makes a product or service top-of-mind, it speaks in shorthand with a slogan or a logo, it makes a promise, and it sings a jingle in your head—until you want to scream!

Karen Post gives us this definition of branding: "The brand is a metal imprint that is earned and belongs to a product, service, organization, individual or event. It's a story embedded in the mind of the market. It's the sum total of the tangible and intangible characteristics of that entity."[1]

Think about where you shop, the services you use, and the products you buy. If a store is well branded, you immediately recognize the sign. Even if you haven't been into that particular location before, you know what to expect when you walk in the door. You probably even recognize the layout. You know right where things are.

At a restaurant chain, you know what you will order before you pull up to the drive-up box, and you know how the food will taste. The sign on the freeway is more than a marker—it is a signal. It reminds you of something, makes your mouth water, and urges you to make an unscheduled stop.

Brands are values and emotion based. They are the sum total of your experiences and expectations of a company, a service, a program, a club, a publication, a destination, a team...or a person.

Your brand is your reputation—an identity—and you have one by design or default. It is what you are known for. It is the imprint of your story on the minds of your market. It is what people think of and how they feel when they see you or hear your name.

Personal brands are definitely in play when a group of managers discuss whom to promote or whom to trust with a critical project. Brands are at work when you interact with your customers, colleagues, employees, and boss. Your brand goes before you when you present your ideas and negotiate for what you need to be successful.

A strong, positive identity is like a key. It opens doors of opportunity and support. It is an endorsement. On the other hand, a weak or negative brand is a lock. It invites low confidence or a lack of cooperation, and resistance from others.

The interesting thing about a brand is that it reinforces itself by attracting behaviors, reactions, and attitudes. If you are known, for example, as a committed, supportive team player, people are more likely to share their ideas and challenges. They give you the key to become an even greater resource.

If you are known as self-promoting and disloyal, people may respond by withholding information and locking you out. The more isolated you are, the more self-preserving you must become to survive.

If your brand is weak or vague, people may not know who you are or what to expect from you. You will not be top-of-mind when exciting opportunities arrive, so you will continue to work behind that veil of ambiguity.

Managing your identity, marketing yourself, and creating a brand and a voice is both a challenge and an opportunity. With some self-analysis you may decide your brand suffers from inconsistency or lack of clarity. Perhaps with one audience your brand is strong and positive, and with another the message is unclear or even negative.

> Cheryl is a midlevel manager with a team of eight direct reports. Without exception these people respect, admire, and trust her. She has developed a reputation with her employees as supportive, outgoing, and capable. This audience gives her positive feedback.
>
> Her peers and higher level managers don't know Cheryl very well. She rarely speaks up in management meetings, and she hasn't built relationships with her colleagues. The feedback from this audience is more of a giant question mark: Who is Cheryl anyway? What does her department do?
>
> Cheryl isn't managing her brand. She is working inside a zone of comfort. She is only confident and dynamic when interacting with her direct reports, and this is a real problem for them, too. Cheryl isn't managing her personal brand *or* the team brand. She is not marketing their results and their value to the rest of the organization. Because she is unknown and ambiguous, her team is, too.

Old Brands Die Hard

Occasionally, in this discussion of branding, women confess they are desperately trying to break free of a negative brand and finding that difficult to do. They've earned a reputation that is blocking the path, and they want, and need, to reinvent themselves. They describe a locked-in feeling when they say, "I am trying to change, but people hold onto those old impressions pretty tightly."

Turning a negative brand into a positive one is difficult, but it can be done. If you find yourself in this situation, be patient with yourself, others, and the process. Brands aren't created instantly, and some impressions leave a permanent mark. You can't erase them. You must replace them with consistently positive impressions. You must invite people to form a new impression—and one invitation won't get the job done.

At first people may not trust the new you. That's fair. With consistency, you will build credibility.

> Marty had created an extremely negative brand for herself. In the midst of a bitter divorce and caring for an elderly parent, she had been unreliable, emotional, and volatile. Marty was known for an unkempt appearance, an angry, defensive attitude, and sloppy work. When she purposed to change that impression, she found it harder than she had imagined.
>
> "The hardest person to influence was the regional manager," Marty admits. "Even though my immediate manager believed in me and my ability to turn the situation around, his boss wasn't convinced. I asked my manager for his advice and support. He found opportunities to market my efforts and highlight my progress. It took months, but with help from my sponsor, I was able to reinvent myself."

Sketch Your Brand

A simple gap analysis will help you understand how strong or weak your current brand is. You may be able to answer these questions on your own, but a little market research is also advised. Ask these questions of yourself and get feedback from your target market to create a balanced perspective. You can do this on a personal level or on a team level. If you lead a team, I encourage you to do both. This is a wonderful teaming exercise.

✓ Who are your target markets—the groups you want to influence with your brand?

✓ What do these people know about you?

✓ What do others think and feel when your name is mentioned—or when they see your number on caller ID?

✓ What would you like your audience to know about you? How do you want them to feel?

✓ How clear and consistent is your brand? Do different groups have different impressions? Where are there inconsistencies in the way you present yourself? What is creating those mixed messages?

✓ What are the points of contact? Where are the opportunities to strengthen your brand and make a positive impression?

✓ How are you maximizing, or missing, those opportunities?

✓ What is your ideal reputation? What do you want to be known for?

✓ What is unique about you? How are you creating a signature style?

✓ What tactics will you use to create a positive, consistent message? What is your marketing plan?

Once you've answered questions like these and completed your market research, pull it all together to sketch the vision of your brand and build a plan of action.

BRAND VISION	TARGET AUDIENCES
• The adjectives you want people to use when describing you • The qualities you want to be most known for • The capabilities you have • What is unique, distinctive, and special about you	• The people you want to "touch" with your brand • Groups you need to influence and impact • People who make the decisions that impact your career opportunities • Individuals, teams, and departments you want to partner with more effectively • Internal and external customers
IMPRESSION POINTS	**TACTICS AND STRATEGIES**
• Points of contact that occur now • Points of contact you need to create or increase the frequency • Instances where people view your work, use what you produce, or are impacted by your processes • Every time you directly or indirectly touch your target audience	• Specific actions you can take to make a clear, consistent imprint • What you will do to demonstrate the characteristics, attributes, and competencies of your brand vision • How you will earn the brand you want to have • How you will live your values and market your message

This branding exercise is an opportunity to organize the ideas you've collected into a focused plan of action. As you design the strategies and tactics that will forge your identity, think about how you can incorporate what you've learned here.

Case studies are scenarios we can learn from, too. Here, you are the case study. If you were to write your story as a business case—complete with your strengths, areas of weakness, challenges, and opportunities—what would the theme be? What would be the greatest teaching points?

If someone were presenting your case to a group of business majors, what observations would they make? What recommendations would they have? What would they learn from your story?

It's an interesting thought, isn't it?

I encourage you to be the case, review your notes, the high-impact ideas, and action items to identify and prioritize your next steps. There may be dozens of ideas that resonate with you. The key is to isolate the ones that will have the most impact for you personally.

As you design your plan, build measurements in. How will you know if you are making progress? What milestones you will look for along the way?

I encourage you to share your branding vision, strategies, and tactics with your mentor or your board of directors. Practice telling your story to the people who are already vested in your success. As you begin to market the message you craft here, remember to manage the message from the inside out.

Speak It

I am a big believer in affirmations—speaking what is powerful and positive into my life, and the lives of others. I believe the ancient power of the blessing is available to us even now. "The LORD will send a *blessing* on your barns and on everything you put your hand to. The LORD your God will bless you in the land he is giving you" (Deuteronomy 28:8, NIV, emphasis added).

I encourage you to turn your goals into positive affirmations and read them aloud every day. Speak them as if they were already true. The following are affirmations you can use to speak the Ten Commandments for Women in the Workplace into your life.

✓ I am designed for success. I have unique strengths and abilities, and my opportunities are waiting for me.

✓ I manage my messages from the inside out. I have an important story to tell, and I tell it well.

✓ I empower myself with options, role clarity, accountability, and optimism.

✓ I am a positive catalyst. I bring solutions.

✓ I equip myself with awareness.

✓ I walk in a spirit of gratitude.

✓ I have the confidence to negotiate. I know what I want, I believe I deserve it, and I feel powerful enough to ask for it.

✓ I lead from my current position by raising the standard and demonstrating extreme initiative.

✓ I am effective even when the people around me are not.

✓ I am strategic.

✓ I secure my future by becoming more valuable and vital. I am building a bridge to my future.

✓ My net will hold.

✓ I turn my stakeholders into shareholders.

✓ I invest in the success of others.

✓ I break through the barriers to establish productive relationships. I turn my adversaries into allies and invite a spirit of collaboration.

✓ I add value to everything I do. I am creative. I am a valuable resource.

✓ I am designed for success, and I am creating a reputation that opens the door of opportunity and unlocks my possibility.

You Were Designed for Success

As I have written this book, I have prayed for the women who will read it. I have prayed for you: That you might find the inspiration, encouragement, and tools you need to release your potential and realize your possibility. That you would discover ideas that help you become more vital and valuable, recognized and rewarded.

This book won't change you or your circumstances. It's what you do with the ideas in this book that will make the difference. In that way, I am honored if I have played even a small part in unfolding your possibility.

I wish you the very best and leave you with this blessing:

May God prosper the work of your hands and the work of your heart;

May you be surrounded by people who will encourage your dreams, celebrate your victories, and if you should forget, remind you who you are;

May the obstacles in your path serve only to equip and strengthen you;

May the difference you make and the value you create be remarkable; and

As you design your life, may the blessings of God overtake you.

High-Impact Ideas

✓ You have an identity by design or by default.

✓ It's not what you know; it's what you do that will make the difference.

✓ Potential is worthless until it is released and realized.

✓ If your brand is weak or vague, people may not know who you are or what to expect from you. You will not be top-of-mind when exciting opportunities arrive, so you will continue to work behind a veil of ambiguity.

✓ Managing your identity, marketing yourself, and creating a brand and a voice is a challenge and an opportunity. With some self-analysis you may decide your brand suffers from inconsistency or lack of clarity. Perhaps with one audience your brand is strong and positive, and with another the message is unclear or even negative.

✓ Turning a negative brand into a positive one is difficult, but it can be done. If you find yourself in this situation, be patient with yourself, others, and the process. Brands aren't created instantly, and some impressions leave a permanent mark. You can't erase them. You must replace them with consistently positive impressions.

✓ Identify your target audience and develop a brand vision.

✓ Build your business case.

✓ Speak what is powerful and positive into your life and the lives of others. The ancient power of the blessing is available to you.

Questions for Reflection

What do you *know* that you don't *do*?

_____

_____

_____

What is your brand, and what is it doing for you?

_____

_____

_____

What are your most important next steps?

_____

_____

_____

Action Items

Identify your target audiences and do some market research.

Develop a sketch of your brand and share it with a mentor or your board of directors.

Write your goals as affirmations and read them aloud every day.

Notes

Chapter 1
The Call to Action

1. Stephanie Chaffins et al., "The Glass Ceiling: Are Women Where They Should Be?" *Education,* March 22, 1995, abstract available at http://www.highbeam.com/doc/1G1-17039288.html (accessed September 17, 2007).
2. Suzanne M. Crampton and Jitendra M. Mishra, "Women in Management," *Public Personnel Management* 28 (1999): 87.
3. Boris B. Baltes and Cara C. Bauer, "Reducing the Effects of Gender Stereotypes on Performance Evaluations," *Sex Roles: A Journal of Research* (November 2002); and Terri Scandura, "Women Can Shatter Job Barriers," *USA Today* (Society for the Advancement of Education), May 1994.
4. A. Elizabeth Lindsey and Walter R. Zakahi, "Women Who Tell and Men Who Ask: Perceptions of Men and Women Departing From Gender Stereotypes During Initial Interaction," *Sex Roles: A Journal of Research* 34 (June 1996).
5. Chaffins et al., "The Glass Ceiling: Are Women Where They Should Be?"
6. Carol T. Schreiber, Karl F. Price, and Ann Morrison, "Workforce Diversity and the Glass Ceiling: Practices, Barriers, Possibilities," *Human Resource Planning* 16 (June 1993).
7. Scandura, "Women Can Shatter Job Barriers."
8. Catherine Fitzgerald and Jennifer Garvey Berger, eds., *Executive Coaching: Practices and Perspectives* (Mountain View, CA: Davies-Black Publishing, 2002).
9. Ram Charan, Stephen Drotter, and James Noel, *The Leadership Pipeline: How to Build the Leadership-Powered Company* (San Francisco: Jossey-Bass, Inc., 2000).

Chapter 2
Commandment 1:
Manage Your Message From the Inside Out

1. Chaffins et al., "The Glass Ceiling: Are Women Where They Should Be?"
2. Stephen R. Covey, *The Seven Habits of Highly Effective People* (New York: Fireside, 1990).
3. Brian Tracy, *Psychology of Achievement* (Niles, IL: Nightingale-Conant, 1998).
4. Kimberly A. Daubman and Harold Sigail, "Gender Differences in Perceptions of How Others Are Affected by Self-Disclosure of Achievement," *Sex Roles: A Journal of Research* 37 (July 1997).
5. Peggy Klaus, *Brag! The Art of Tooting Your Own Horn Without Blowing It* (New York: Warner Business Books, 2003), 18–19.

6. Lawrence B. Stein and Stanley L. Brodsky, "When Infants Wail: Frustration and Gender as Variables in Distress Disclosure," *Journal of General Psychology* 122, no. 1 (1995): 19–27.

7. Bert Decker, *High Impact Communication* (Niles, IL: Nightingale-Conant, 1992).

Chapter 3
Commandment 2:
Empower Yourself—What Are You Waiting For?

1. Adapted from Jack Canfield and Jacqueline Miller, *Heart at Work* (Columbus, OH: McGraw-Hill, 1996).

2. Matthew 25:14–30.

3. "Accountability," Dictionary.com, *The American Heritage Dictionary of the English Language, Fourth Edition*, Houghton Mifflin Company, 2004, http://dictionary.reference.com/browse/accountability (accessed September 20, 2007).

4. Roger Connors, Tom Smith, and Craig Hickman, *The Oz Principle: Getting Results Through Individual and Organizational Accountability* (New Jersey: Prentice Hall Press, 1994).

5. John G. Miller, *Flipping the Switch: Unleash the Power of Personal Accountability Using the QBQ!* (New York: The Penguin Group, 2006), 10.

6. Jeff Davidson, "Optimism in an Era of Uncertainty," *Public Management*, November 2004.

7. Jim Collins, *Good to Great: Why Some Companies Make the Leap…and Others Don't* (New York: HarperBusiness, 2001), 199.

8. Martin E. P. Seligman, PhD, *Learned Optimism: How to Change Your Mind and Your Life* (New York: Pocket Books, 1990, 1998).

9. Jack Canfield, Mark Victor Hansen, and Les Hewitt, *The Power of Focus: How to Hit Your Business, Personal and Financial Targets With Absolute Certainty* (Deerfield Beach, FL: HCI, 2000).

10. Covey, *The Seven Habits of Highly Effective People*.

Chapter 4
Commandment 3:
Equip Yourself With Awareness

1. Adele B. Lynn, *The EQ Difference: A Powerful Plan for Putting Emotional Intelligence to Work* (New York: AMACOM, a division of American Management Association, 2005).

2. Adapted from Consortium for Research on Emotional Intelligence in Organizations, "Emotional Competence Framework: Personal Competence," http://www.eiconsortium.org/research/emotional_competence_framework .htm (accessed August 29, 2007).

3. Thomas Stirr, *Miller's Bolt: A Modern Business Parable* (New York: Basic Books, 1997).

4. Covey, *The Seven Habits of Highly Effective People*, 242.

Chapter 5
Commandment 4:
Become a Skilled Negotiator

1. Linda Babcock and Sara Laschever, *Women Don't Ask: Negotiation and the Gender Divide* (Princeton, NJ: Princeton University Press, 2003).
2. Roger Fisher, William Ury, and Bruce Patton, *Getting to Yes: Negotiating Agreement Without Giving In,* 2nd ed. (New York: Penguin Books, 1991).
3. Ibid.
4. Richard E. Walton and Robert B. McKersie, *A Behavioral Theory of Labor Negotiations: An Analysis of a Social Interaction System* (New York: McGraw-Hill, Inc., 1965).
5. Fisher, Ury, and Patton, *Getting to Yes.*
6. Allan R. Cohen and David L. Bradford, *Influence Without Authority* (New York: John Wiley & Sons, Inc., 1989, 1991).

Chapter 6
Commandment 5:
Lead From Your Current Position

1. John C. Maxwell, *The 360-Degree Leader: Developing Your Influence From Anywhere in the Organization* (Nashville, TN: Thomas Nelson, Inc., 2005).
2. "City of Irving, TX, Strategic Plan and Phases," The City of Irving, Texas, http://www.cityofirving.org/text-only/Irving/inspections/strategic-plans .html (accessed August 31, 2007).

Chapter 8
Commandment 7:
Think Like a Project Manager

1. Eric Verzuh, *The Fast Forward MBA in Project Management,* 2nd ed. (Hoboken, NJ: John Wiley & Sons, Inc., 2005).
2. Project Management Institute, Inc., *A Guide to the Project Management Body of Knowledge* (Newton Square, PA: Project Management Institute, Inc., 2004).
3. Ibid.
4. Michael M. Lombardo, EdD, and Robert W. Eichinger, PhD, *FYI: For Your Improvement,* 4th ed. (Minneapolis, MN: Lominger Limited, Inc., 2004).

Chapter 9
Commandment 8:
Invest in the Success of Others

1. Matthew McKay, PhD, Martha Davis, PhD, and Patrick Fanning, *Messages: The Communication Skills Book,* 2nd ed. (Oakland, CA: New Harbinger Publications, Inc., 1995).

Chapter 10
Commandment 9:
Break Through the Barriers

1. Patrick Lencioni, *Silos, Politics, and Turf Wars: A Leadership Fable About Destroying the Barriers That Turn Colleagues Into Competitors* (San Francisco, CA: Jossey-Bass, 2006).
2. Decker, *High Impact Communication.*

Chapter 12
Answering the Call

1. Karen Post, *Brain Tattoos: Creating Unique Brands That Stick in Your Customers' Minds* (New York: AMACOM, a division of American Management Association, 2004).

If you enjoyed this book and would like to find out more about Dondi Scumaci, her speaking dates, and other resources that are available, please visit **www.dondiscumaci.com**. At the Web site you'll be able to interact with Dondi through her blog; purchase CDs, mentoring resources, and DVDs; and tap into a wealth of tools and information designed to help you succeed in business.

STOP BY TODAY TO FIND OUT MORE.

dondi SCUMACI.inc

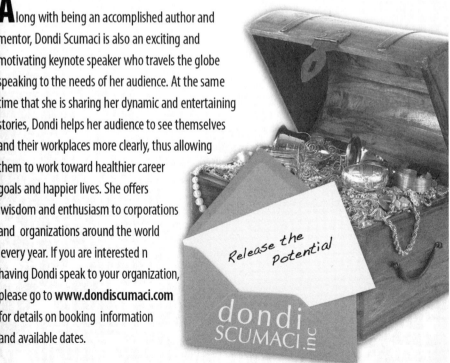

Along with being an accomplished author and mentor, Dondi Scumaci is also an exciting and motivating keynote speaker who travels the globe speaking to the needs of her audience. At the same time that she is sharing her dynamic and entertaining stories, Dondi helps her audience to see themselves and their workplaces more clearly, thus allowing them to work toward healthier career goals and happier lives. She offers wisdom and enthusiasm to corporations and organizations around the world every year. If you are interested n having Dondi speak to your organization, please go to **www.dondiscumaci.com** for details on booking information and available dates.